LARGE PRINT

Crossword Puzzle Book for Adults

Volume 2

D0943161

For more fun puzzle books
visit our Amazon store!

For US Puzzlers: bit.ly/rosenbladt
For UK Puzzlers: bit.ly/rosenbladt-uk
For CA Puzzlers: bit.ly/rosenbladt-ca

Puzzle 1

ACROSS
1. Stepped
6. Reveal secret
10. Male deer
14. Course
15. ___ Martin (cognac)
16. Divan
17. Available
18. A long, long time
19. "East of Eden" brother
20. Methodism
23. Calendar abbr.
24. "___ pig's eye!"
25. Us
27. Spiny ant-eaters
32. Window ledge
33. Myrna of "The Thin Man"
34. Slink
36. Gannet
39. Two-up bats
41. Prophets
43. Wait
44. Mountain nymph
46. Isabella, por ejemplo
48. Not
49. Public disturbance
51. Author of psalms
53. Gauzelike papers
56. Mamie's man
57. Knock with knuckles
58. Sac in which bile is stored
64. Officiating priest of a mosque
66. Variety
67. Be still, at sea
68. Opening run
69. Lines of thought, for short?
70. Mountaineer's tool
71. Falsehoods
72. Minor oath
73. Weakling

DOWN
1. Front of ship
2. First class (1-3)
3. Intersects
4. And more
5. Relies (on)
6. La ___ Tar Pits
7. Boxer Spinks
8. Prenatal test, for short
9. Ancient cloth
10. F.I.C.A. funds it
11. Trattoria treat
12. In an entangled state
13. Swindler
21. Tugs
22. Dr.'s orders
26. Untidy person
27. Nevada city
28. Coconut husk fibre
29. Space beyond three dimensions
30. Teacher of Heifetz
31. Slumber
35. Malay dagger
37. Nabokov heroine and others
38. Nair competitor
40. "Je ne ___ quoi"
42. Gastropod mollusk
45. Cricketer, - Walters
47. Acid neutralizers
50. Having nipples
52. Noble Italian family name
53. Ordeal
54. Poets' feet
55. More wily
59. Kraft Nabisco Championship org.
60. Elite
61. Bad marks
62. Flight data, briefly
63. Classic theater name
65. "ER" roles

2

Puzzle 2

ACROSS

1. Combined
6. Barbed comments
10. Looped handle
14. Television repeat
15. Carrier whose name means "skyward"
16. Soft shoes
17. 8th letter
18. Wind instrument
19. Asian nurse
20. Bondage
23. Island (France)
24. "Bambi" character
25. Fine threads
27. Portrayed
32. Print tint
33. "Catch-22" pilot
34. Downy duck
36. Bristles
39. Like a 911 call: Abbr.
41. Young bird
43. Terza ___ (Italian verse form)
44. Radioactive gaseous element
46. La ___
48. Vessel or duct
49. Smart - , show-off

51. Hungry, greedy
53. Impure
56. Decade
57. "Vive le ___!"
58. Result of realizing
64. Boys in the 'hood
66. Strike breaker
67. Novelist Cather
68. Lago contents
69. First word of the "Aeneid"
70. Gallic girlfriends
71. Nidus
72. Back
73. Leaven

DOWN

1. "Dies ___" (hymn)
2. Düsseldorf denial
3. Food scraps
4. Central parts
5. Embellish
6. Ballet jump
7. Astringent
8. Infants
9. Slopes
10. Doc bloc
11. Denoting a case
12. Burn with water
13. Australia vs England cricket trophy
21. Oracular
22. "___ bien!"

26. Little, e.g.
27. Performer
28. "Aunt" with a "Cope Book"
29. Rapacious
30. Old English letters
31. Free of ice
35. Some TV's
37. Quote, part 2
38. The Orient
40. Trundle
42. Awkward person
45. Never
47. Passageway between buildings
50. Roman general
52. Eventually
53. Metropolitan
54. Norwegian name of Norway
55. Mother-of-pearl
59. Tibetan monk
60. Bridge support
61. Hip bones
62. Arena shouts
63. Political cartoonist called "our best recruiting sergeant" by Lincoln
65. Took a seat

4

Puzzle 3

ACROSS
1. Developed
6. Valley
10. Trans-Siberian Railroad city
14. Aegean region
15. ___ Bator, Mongolia
16. French chef's mushroom
17. Dens
18. Eager
19. Land measure
20. Jointed or segmented
23. Babe
24. Beak
25. Measurement in yards
27. Identify a disease
32. Riding strap
33. S.A.S.E., e.g.
34. Be silent
36. Ancient Roman magistrate
39. Maturing agent
41. Prefix, turbine
43. Wood sorrels
44. Critic, at times
46. Botch
48. Halifax clock setting: Abbr.
49. Chemical endings
51. Letters
53. Repaints
56. ___-Foy, Que.
57. Dockworker's org.
58. Instrumental
64. Openwork fabric
66. Visage
67. Home of the Black Bears
68. Weave wool
69. Fibber
70. Bits
71. Icelandic epic
72. "Enchanted" girl in a 2004 film
73. Minor oath

DOWN
1. Venomous lizard
2. Lion's call
3. "Don't bet ___!"
4. Fitting with cables
5. Beginning to exist
6. Twofold
7. Edison's middle name
8. Non-clergy
9. Make beloved
10. Wood sorrel
11. Automatic
12. Young child (Colloq)
13. Nancy Drew's creator
21. German submarine (1-4)
22. Endure
26. Lover of Aeneas
27. Precious
28. "Young Frankenstein" woman
29. Constituent of vinegar
30. Offscourings
31. Weird
35. Cookbook abbr.
37. Cut with laser
38. Ballpark figs.
40. U.S. divorce city
42. Writer of lyric poetry
45. Quantity of paper
47. Bonelike
50. Smother
52. Great fear
53. "Duino Elegies" poet
54. African antelope
55. Garden pest
59. Suffix with poet
60. "Buona ___" (Italian greeting)
61. Jot
62. Biol. subject
63. Profit failure
65. Greek letter

ACROSS

1. "American Buffalo" playwright
6. Wing: Prefix
10. People in charge: Abbr.
14. Overjoy
15. Australian explorer
16. Intestinal parts
17. Quotes
18. Heroic
19. Pesky insects
20. Crushed with sorrow
23. Make lace
24. Actress Vardalos of "My Big Fat Greek Wedding"
25. Skillfully
27. Costs of running businesses
32. A Great Lake
33. "Gloria in excelsis ___"
34. Fish organs
36. Gumbo vegetables
39. Sea eagle
41. Slangy greetings
43. Merit
44. Knob-like
46. Waned
48. Bind
49. Always
51. Free from dirt
53. Augur
56. Simple fastener
57. An age
58. Skillfully manipulating someone
64. Labels
66. Prefix, air
67. Scout unit
68. "It was ___ mistake!"
69. "Aha!"
70. Prefix, four
71. English court
72. Former Fords
73. Dutch exports

DOWN

1. Field for an engr.
2. "I cannot tell ___"
3. ___ Hari
4. Eternal (Poet)
5. Examining
6. Equal
7. Typographical error
8. Eleniak of "Baywatch"
9. Ebb
10. Time div.
11. Beautiful people
12. Iron, lead, or copper
13. Flavoursome
21. Fundamental
22. Fiddling Roman emperor
26. Spear point
27. Paradise
28. Prefix, dry
29. Worth serious consideration
30. "Night" author Wiesel
31. Thick slices
35. Japanese noodles
37. Mex. neighbor
38. Bygone blade
40. Roof overhang
42. Sanity
45. Literally, "injured"
47. Small dining room
50. Refasten timber
52. Covered with pitch
53. Kind of position
54. Papal vestment
55. Excrete
59. Angered
60. Denials
61. Very small quantity
62. Standard
63. Transcript stats
65. Posed

Puzzle 5

ACROSS

1. Conductor Georg
6. Helen's mother, in Greek myth
10. Gardner and others
14. Lake Geneva spa
15. Martinique et Guadeloupe
16. Assist
17. Police informers
18. Girl
19. Opera solo
20. Somnambulist
23. Soldiers
24. Golf peg
25. Not straight
27. Move to a new place
32. ___ II (razor brand)
33. Medical suffix
34. Armistice
36. Soccer star Michelle
39. III
41. Lightweight overgarment
43. Nautical, below
44. "Mefistofele" role
46. "McSorley's Bar" painter
48. "Love Story" composer Francis
49. Geom. shape
51. Jostling
53. Roman magistrate
56. Ear: Prefix
57. Soak flax
58. Tractable
64. "Get ___!"
66. Fraternal gp.
67. On fire
68. "Hercules" spinoff
69. Great age
70. Rebind
71. Burglar
72. Refuse
73. Upright

DOWN

1. Burns and Allen: Abbr.
2. Egg-shaped
3. Italian currency
4. Start liking
5. Examine
6. Wallace of Reader's Digest
7. Airline since 1948
8. Writing tables
9. Agree
10. Exclamation of surprise
11. Very fine pasta
12. Foreign
13. Exactly
21. Erodes
22. Singular, to Caesar
26. New Zealand parrot
27. Fragrant flower
28. Disney's "___ and the Detectives"
29. Tearing
30. Rolaids rival
31. Sorbonne, e.g.
35. Biol. branch
37. Brown and white horse
38. A drink
40. Leg joint
42. Shish ___
45. Pituitary hormone
47. Medium, maybe
50. "What a shame"
52. Low-frequency loudspeaker
53. Deputy
54. "Walk Away ___" (1966 hit)
55. Indian currency
59. Anon
60. Choosing-up word
61. Bird of prey
62. Clapton who sang "Layla"
63. Hair removal brand
65. Label

11

Puzzle 6

ACROSS

1. Jeans fabric
6. Cough syrup amts.
10. Rent-a-car company
14. Like Bo-Peep's charges
15. Related
16. Scene of first miracle
17. Bogotá babies
18. Mature
19. Peruse
20. Leaping insect
23. Diminutive suffix
24. "Sprechen ___ Deutsch?"
25. Member of the mustard family
27. Fitted new back parts to shoes
32. A join
33. "___ Believer"
34. Requite
36. Trench
39. Exclude
41. Stair post
43. Lubricate
44. Wheel covers
46. Caught congers
48. Scottish hill
49. Auto import
51. Railway ties
53. Type of pill
56. IV amounts
57. Hart Trophy winner, 1970-72
58. Sensible
64. Train track
66. African river
67. "Be-Bop-___" (Gene Vincent hit)
68. Adolescent pimples
69. Small amounts, as of cream
70. Refine my melting
71. ___-mutton
72. Dagger
73. S-bends

DOWN

1. Hit or punch (Colloq)
2. At any time
3. One of Columbus's ships
4. Actually existing
5. More untidy
6. Polynesian root food
7. Jump
8. Browning title character
9. Derides
10. Coolers, briefly
11. Electron tube
12. As a whole
13. Arabian capital
21. Trojan beauty
22. Regretted
26. Feminine name
27. Uproar
28. U.S. TV award
29. Spring used for timepiece
30. Fencing sword
31. Coolidge's veep
35. Shout
37. "Good buddy"
38. Female birds
40. After-dinner selection
42. Blood sucker
45. First king of Israel
47. Die
50. Mixes
52. Hymns
53. Polyp colony
54. "It's ___ against time"
55. Perrier rival
59. Dresden's river
60. ___-majeste
61. Club fees
62. Australian super-model
63. Bygone auto
65. Zodiac sign

ACROSS
1. Slightly drunk
6. Warner Bros. creation
10. Prefix, eight
14. Ammonia derivative
15. Actor Cronyn
16. Cartoonist Addams
17. "He's ___ nowhere man" (Beatles lyric)
18. Go-aheads
19. Nervous twitches
20. Colonies
23. Never, in Neuss
24. Spanish hero
25. Chooses
27. Loftiness
32. Sprint
33. Alfonso XIII's queen
34. Goblin
36. Wicket cross-pieces
39. Abbr. on an envelope
41. Condiment
43. It means "red" in Mongolian
44. Great fear
46. Relatively cool sun
48. Soap ingredient
49. "Fish Magic" painter
51. Catcher's position
53. Bosoms
56. Part of E.E.C.: Abbr.
57. Abbr. in a help wanted ad
58. Exist together
64. Bowser's bowlful
66. Seine sights
67. Pitchers
68. Profound
69. Floor covering
70. Attack
71. Classify
72. Richard of "A Summer Place"
73. Expels

DOWN
1. Familia members
2. 2002 Literature Nobelist Kertesz
3. Saucy person
4. Grab
5. Shouting
6. Those
7. Yorkshire river
8. Portents
9. Fit together
10. Columbus Day mo.
11. Silvery gray fur rodent
12. Implied
13. Donkeys
21. Paradises
22. Thick slice
26. Son of Isaac and Rebekah
27. Principal
28. Foreword: Abbr.
29. Monitor
30. Saturate
31. Compress
35. Opposite of endo-
37. Puts down
38. Large knife
40. "The Lion King" lion
42. Chair designer Charles
45. Fam. tree member
47. Noted news agency
50. Star (Heraldry)
52. Concoct
53. Necklace
54. Loggers' contest
55. Baseball commissioner Bud
59. Lucy Lawless role
60. "Help ___ the way!"
61. Hawaiian goose
62. Bird's crop
63. Guesses: Abbr.
65. Choose

15

ACROSS
1. Small violin
6. Sounds of disapproval
10. ___ Mujeres, Mexico
14. Poplar
15. Wings
16. Sgts., e.g.
17. Gibe
18. "Jour de Fete" star
19. Taxis
20. Reduce to a system
23. "The Raven" author
24. Charlotte-to-Raleigh dir.
25. Weirdest
27. Twice a year
32. Damn
33. Like some stocks, for short
34. Awry
36. Glacial ice formation
39. Turner and others
41. Swiss mountain
43. Mideast capital
44. Diplomat Root
46. Batty
48. Geom. figure
49. "___ chance!"
51. Kerb
53. Length in feet

56. Prefix, before
57. Sick
58. Trotting race
64. Teutonic turndown
66. Debatable
67. Wearies
68. Actress Winslet
69. Notion
70. Organic compounds
71. Old dagger
72. Prison room
73. Search for water

DOWN
1. Brewery equipment
2. "___, old chap"
3. Musical work
4. Suitable for Lent
5. Aerial
6. Good-bye (2-2)
7. Lath
8. Couric of "Today"
9. Taken
10. "Murder, ___"
11. Persistent rascal
12. American grey wolves
13. Thing of value
21. North Sea tributary
22. Periods of history
26. Chemical suffixes
27. Skeletal part

28. Emphatic type: Abbr.
29. Variety of amphibole
30. Related by blood
31. Assistance in climbing or mounting something (3-2)
35. Scorpion-like N.Z. insect
37. Has ___ with
38. Dray
40. Fired a gun
42. Replies to an invitation, briefly
45. American state
47. Unit of magnetic intensity
50. Asexual
52. Sheep variety
53. Rats
54. City on the Allegheny
55. Wear away
59. Christmas
60. And others, for short
61. In a line
62. Art collectibles
63. "___ quam videri" (North Carolina's motto)
65. Born

ACROSS

1. Wearer of three stars: Abbr.
6. Ponder
10. "Garfield" dog
14. African antelope
15. On ___ (equipotent)
16. Lighting gas
17. Dame Nellie -
18. 1814 Byron poem
19. One's parents (Colloq)
20. Vision defect
23. Acknowledgement of debt
24. No
25. In view
27. Plantain weed
32. Cupola
33. C.I.O.'s partner
34. "The Brady Bunch" housekeeper
36. Hospital rooms
39. Cambridge colleges, for short
41. South American beast
43. New Mexico art community
44. Kudrow and Bonet
46. Aligned
48. Young child
49. Snare
51. Trying people
53. Twinkled
56. British verb ending
57. Knight's title
58. Choice cut of beef
64. Appendage
66. Links numbers
67. Ant
68. Years abroad
69. Neeson of "Kinsey"
70. Capital of Morocco
71. Torn clothing
72. "Momo" author Michael
73. Sleeping noise

DOWN

1. ___ Linda, Calif.
2. "___ chic"
3. Golden
4. Waning
5. American waterfall
6. ___ fide
7. ___ the crack of dawn
8. Hindu garments
9. Rubbed out
10. Yoko -
11. Intentional
12. Iodine solution
13. Follow
21. Wattle species
22. Sound of a cat
26. Amo, amas, ___
27. Actor Julia
28. Sidi ___, Morocco
29. Scorching
30. River deposit
31. Frighten
35. Flightless flock
37. Entrance
38. Jet-setters' jets, once
40. "___ Smile" (1976 hit)
42. Race of Norse gods
45. Coarsely ground corn
47. Sprinters
50. Persons in general
52. Naval clerk
53. The Sun, for example
54. Climbing vine
55. Sap
59. Type of jazz
60. Salinger dedicatee
61. Boss on a shield
62. Scorch
63. Suffix, diminutive
65. Sue Grafton's "___ for Lawless"

Puzzle 10

ACROSS
1. Skeleton
6. Driving shower
10. Bothers
14. Heavens: Prefix
15. River in central Switzerland
16. Apollo astronaut Slayton
17. Rugby formation
18. Prejudice
19. Coal-rich German region
20. Powerfully binding
23. Economic stat.
24. Cathedral city
25. Stretchy
27. Rockets
32. Pith helmet
33. Dined
34. Finnish architect Alvar ___
36. 3 Banked money
39. Repair
41. "Mr. Belvedere" actress Graff
43. Compel
44. Arab leader
46. Healthcare benefits giant
48. Golfers mound
49. Great quantity
51. Having no roof
53. Engraved
56. Corp. bigwig
57. You, abroad
58. Translated clearly
64. Lengthy
66. Level to ground
67. Adult
68. Basics
69. Future doc's exam
70. ___ Circus (where St. Peter was crucified)
71. Greet
72. A dog's age
73. Singer Lopez

DOWN
1. Kiss
2. Killer whale
3. Narcotics agent
4. Accustoms
5. Republic on the E coast of Africa
6. "Quién ___?"
7. First son of Adam and Eve
8. Salt of uric acid
9. Remove the salt from
10. Commercials
11. Render (a bomb) inoperative
12. Giraffe-like animal
13. Chinese
21. Massacre site of 1968
22. South-east Asian nation
26. Junk E-mail
27. "If He Walked Into My Life" musical
28. A particular
29. Old age
30. "The Intimate ___" (1990 jazz album)
31. Direct
35. Upon
37. Supplements
38. Barely passing grades
40. Metric prefix
42. Methuselah's father
45. Grate
47. Insult
50. "Goodness!"
52. An idler
53. Moslem religion
54. Zeus changed her to stone
55. Harsh Athenian lawgiver
59. Islamic call to prayer
60. Guinea pigs, maybe
61. Hindu garment
62. Designer von Furstenberg
63. First name in 50's TV
65. Clock std.

Puzzle 10

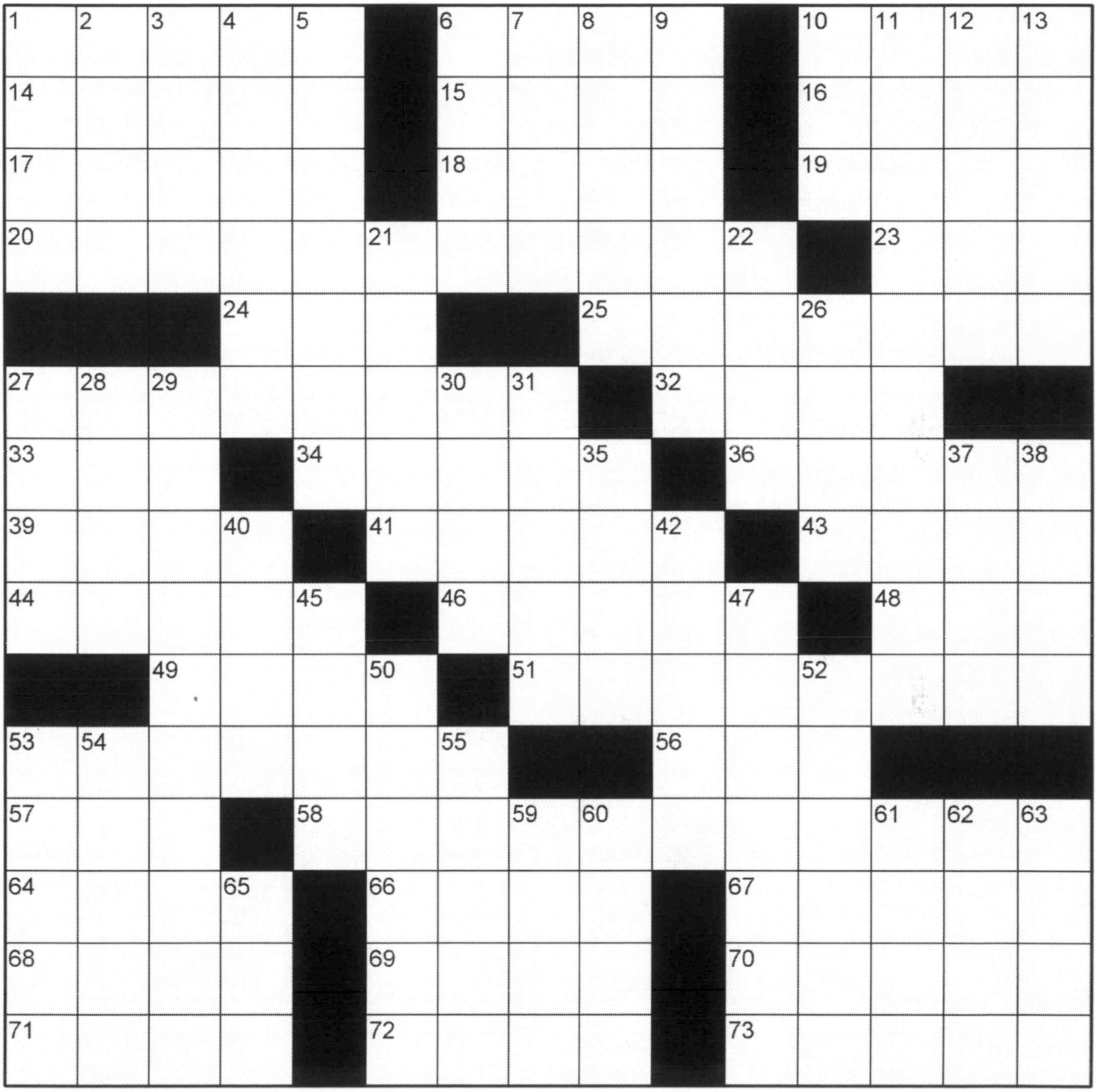

Puzzle 11

ACROSS
1. Beg
6. Nutritional info
10. Chi hrs.
13. Bizarre
14. Jazz (up)
15. Unconsciousness
16. Place where washing can be taken to be done
18. One having second thoughts
19. George Sand's "Elle et ___"
20. Upswept hairdo
21. Dresses which flare from the top (1-5)
23. Pinnacle
24. "No bid"
25. Spreads
28. Food fish
31. Disorderly flights
32. Drink noisily
33. Sheltered side
34. Bones, anatomically
35. Asunder
36. Menlo Park middle name
37. Slowing, in mus.
38. Nitrogen compound
39. Introduction
40. Maddening
42. Oyster gems
43. Female relatives
44. Ringlet
45. Actress Dolores
47. Nipples
48. Pioneer cell phone co.
51. Others, to Ovid
52. Bloodthirsty
55. Welt
56. "Aha"
57. Smooth transition
58. Grandmother
59. Potato (Colloq)
60. Coarse woollen fabric

DOWN
1. Election
2. Hawaiian feast
3. Sewing case
4. Prince Valiant's son
5. Subtracts
6. ___ Island
7. Major-___
8. Alias
9. Isolate
10. Adviser
11. "Peter Pan" role
12. Sailors
15. Brittle
17. Tach readings
22. Scandinavian
23. "The Thin Man" canine
24. Habituate
25. Frosty
26. Red dye
27. Of our country
28. Jargon
29. Roister
30. Join lines
32. Reels
35. Simple cell division
36. ___ Sea (Amu Darya's outlet)
38. Lambs: Lat.
39. Continue
41. Pertaining to the ear
42. Kind of platter
44. Behind bars
45. Daybreak
46. Parmenides' home
47. French tire
48. Challenge
49. Genuine
50. Looked over
53. Egyptian serpent
54. Novel

Puzzle 12

ACROSS
1. Slangy greetings
6. The maple
10. Brassiere
13. Bird of Celtic lore
14. Dear, as a signorina
15. Carrier whose name means "skyward"
16. Leaving to live in another country
18. Table salt, to a chemist
19. "Dilbert" cartoonist Scott Adams has one: Abbr.
20. Religious image: Var.
21. Butchers' offerings
23. Has ___ with
24. Smock
25. Defame
28. Stealers of game
31. Irish county
32. "A Woman Called ___" (Emmy-winning TV movie)
33. Cardinal number
34. Elapse
35. Certain navel
36. Actress Sorvino
37. "Another Green World" composer
38. Is ___ (probably will)
39. Increase
40. Weirdness
42. Pretends
43. New York's ___ Fisher Hall
44. Jetty
45. Worldly goods
47. Hang
48. Exclamation of surprise
51. Subatomic particle
52. Fib
55. Gumbo
56. Old Chinese money
57. Nobelist Bohr
58. Timid
59. Serpents
60. Eminent

DOWN
1. Mr. Miniver in "Mrs. Miniver"
2. Foot
3. Opera solo
4. Dot follower
5. Cleansing injection
6. Follow, as a tip
7. First son of Adam and Eve
8. Sea eagle
9. Fashion industry
10. Covering
11. Sprint contest
12. "___ fair in love and war"
15. Methuselah's father
17. Related by blood
22. ___ Grande, Fla.
23. Well ventilated
24. Book leaf
25. John D. MacDonald sleuth Travis ___
26. Solo
27. Place where experiments take place
28. "Designing Women" co-star
29. Television repeat
30. Breaks suddenly
32. Courageous
35. Short musical drama
36. Naturalist John
38. Without ___ (daringly)
39. Convex fluting
41. Ex of the Donald
42. Locate
44. Bell ringings
45. Epic poetry
46. Hindu sect
47. Prepare patient for operation
48. "Zip-___-Doo-Dah"
49. ___ breve
50. Publishing giant
53. Small batteries
54. Board member: Abbr.

ACROSS

1. African musical instrument
6. Droops
10. Big TV maker
13. Poet W. H. ___
14. "Q ___ queen"
15. Length measures
16. Make slim
18. Capital of Western Samoa
19. Airline to Amsterdam
20. "Shave ___ haircut"
21. Abroad
23. 1961 space chimp
24. Penniless
25. "Fiddler on the Roof" setting
28. Halves
31. Football Hall-of-Famer Greasy ___
32. Graf rival
33. Faucet
34. The "E" of B.P.O.E.
35. Rage
36. "Thank Heaven for Little Girls" musical
37. Mature
38. Smart - , show-offs
39. Drudge
40. Inhabitant of Kashmir
42. Trimmed tree branches
43. - Rock, Uluru
44. Bit
45. Notch
47. Item of footwear
48. 1972 treaty subj.
51. Willingly
52. Not possible
55. Hindu god of destruction
56. Broten of hockey fame
57. Gogol's "___ Bulba"
58. Metal-bearing mineral
59. Brave
60. Shatter

DOWN

1. Face cover
2. Papal edict
3. As previously given
4. "In the Good Old Summertime" lyricist Shields
5. Moderately slow
6. Gemstones
7. Continent
8. Dogfaces
9. More underhanded
10. Iteration
11. Line roof
12. Just barely
15. Lacking brightness
17. Chemical compound
22. Cries of disgust
23. Long fish
24. Performances by one
25. Move stealthily
26. Andrew Wyeth's "___ Pictures"
27. Plummets
28. French. thank you
29. Bird of prey
30. Glimpsed
32. Court figures
35. Trifling
36. Larva
38. Prayer ending
39. Clergymen
41. Laughing dog
42. Things in favour of something
44. Wild Asian dog
45. Assuming that's true
46. Neet rival
47. Junk E-mail
48. Magician's opening
49. "Gil ___"
50. Network
53. "Give ___ break!"
54. Braggart (Colloq) (1.2)

ACROSS
1. Jewish lawgiver
6. Complacent
10. Obese
13. Egg producer
14. Mandlikova of tennis
15. Govern
16. Eggplants
18. Abbr. at the end of a list
19. "Trust ___" (1937 hit)
20. Holly
21. Thick
23. Like a line, briefly
24. Blur
25. Defame
28. Cowering
31. Banish
32. "Mule Train" singer, 1949
33. Male offspring
34. Is victorious
35. Door swinger
36. "___ boy!"
37. 1997 U.S. Open champ
38. Skeleton
39. Oust
40. Became more intense
42. Distinctive ages
43. First name in rock
44. Talon
45. Destroyer
47. Philippine island
48. Diving bird
51. Nourishment
52. Prophetic revelation
55. "Miss ___ Regrets"
56. "Me neither"
57. Artist's stand
58. French seasoning
59. Face
60. Hamlet

DOWN
1. Groan
2. Egg
3. "Quién ___?"
4. Before
5. Cleansing injection
6. Baulked
7. Tailless cat
8. A abroad
9. Petrol
10. Ahead of the times
11. Woe is me
12. Prefix, distant
15. Relabel
17. Valley
22. Prefix, well
23. Lubricates
24. Ship's prisons
25. Spoke Persian?
26. Of an axis
27. Flaxseed oil
28. Thrashed
29. Nick
30. Biting insects
32. Napery
35. Recipient of an honor
36. Confess
38. "La Belle et la ___"
39. Shoulder ornament
41. Walks wearily
42. Exile isle
44. Rhodes of Rhodesia
45. Roswell sightings
46. Musical symbol
47. "The Last of the Mohicans" girl
48. Lhasa ___
49. Consumer
50. Large seaweed
53. Flax ball
54. Exclamation of disgust

Puzzle 15

ACROSS
1. Let loose
6. Infant's carriage
10. ___ al-Khaimah (one of the United Arab Emirates)
13. Poker Flat chronicler
14. The villain in Othello
15. Ernie's "Sesame Street" pal
16. Consisting of a single chamber
18. Peak
19. Pig
20. Roster
21. Cyclotron inventor ___ Lawrence
23. Boxer Oscar ___ Hoya
24. Driving showers
25. Purpose
28. Gesture of approval
31. Tam
32. Loops
33. Kamoze of reggae
34. Spoken
35. Chili con ___
36. Fly larvae
37. Fleet runner: Abbr.
38. Centre of attention
39. "Enough!"
40. Russian empresses
42. Sailor's forward cabin
43. Mexican silverwork center
44. Hyperbolic sine
45. Book of elementary principles
47. Count played by Jim Carrey in "Lemony Snicket's A Series of Unfortunate Events"
48. Cole Porter's "___ Clown"
51. Lock part fitted to staple
52. State of being highly aroused
55. Performs
56. Side
57. "Orphée" painter
58. French possessive
59. Gaelic
60. Works hard

DOWN
1. "Don't think so"
2. Prefix meaning "one-billionth"
3. Prude
4. Etcetera
5. Closest
6. Michelangelo masterpiece
7. ___ avis
8. ___ Khan
9. Small particle
10. Economic downturns
11. 3 Weapons
12. Printer's mark, keep
15. Getaway destination, maybe
17. Breakwater
22. Jamaican exports
23. Grudge fight
24. Leg parts
25. Torpedo vessel (1-4)
26. Jocks' antitheses
27. Playwrights
28. Doughnut-shaped surface
29. Till
30. Ski course
32. Chocolate nut
35. Substantial
36. German composer
38. Set, in Somme
39. Construct
41. Sloping walkways
42. Decree
44. Ooze
45. Excellent, in modern slang
46. Sprint contest
47. Wood sorrels
48. When repeated, a vitamin B deficiency
49. Chemical compound
50. Firm parts: Abbr.
53. Gen ___
54. Cattle low

Puzzle 16

ACROSS

1. Euripides drama
6. "The Thin Man" dog
10. City in NW Iran
13. Habituate
14. Transcript stats
15. "Star Trek" helmsman
16. Difficulty in speech
18. Golf mounds
19. Drunkard
20. Absent
21. Car shed
23. Fraternity letters
24. Upbeat
25. Moon of Mars
28. More slushy
31. Underwater navigational aid
32. Alone
33. "The Steve Allen Show" regular
34. Architect William Van ___
35. Hoisted, nautically
36. Lake
37. Meadow
38. Gravelly hillside
39. Corrective eye surgery
40. Fictitious
42. Gentlemen: Abbr.
43. Greek writer of fables
44. Campus military org.
45. Star in Aquila
47. Thin rope
48. Vietnam
51. Female servant
52. Study of demons
55. 24-hr. conveniences
56. Gen. follower
57. Broaden
58. "___ Haw"
59. Lairs
60. Monetary unit of Nigeria

DOWN

1. Drugs, briefly
2. Greek war goddess
3. Fine dry soil
4. Period of history
5. Bubbler
6. Turkish generals
7. Agile
8. - Chi. Slow moving martial art form
9. Together
10. Funny feeling
11. Cassini of fashion
12. Think
15. Denude
17. It was
22. Egyptian serpents
23. "Voice of Israel" author
24. "Kate & ___"
25. Hymn
26. Like Swiss cheese
27. In single file
28. The New Yorker cartoonist Edward
29. Monetary unit of Iceland
30. Smells foul
32. Leather strip
35. Granted
36. Gender abbr.
38. Spanish words of agreement (2.2)
39. A disappointment (3-4)
41. Flip response?
42. Morning
44. Land measures
45. Chinese nurse
46. Overdue
47. "Follow me!"
48. Knots
49. Maturing agent
50. Talking bird
53. Computer file suffix
54. ___ Fail (Irish coronation stone)

Puzzle 17

ACROSS

1. Staid
6. Sovereign
10. Endings to some e-mails
13. Stage
14. Type of inflorescence
15. Steal
16. Diplomatic official
18. At sea
19. Code-cracking org.
20. Pipe
21. Eye parts: Var.
23. Snake sound
24. French story
25. Church laws
28. Theatrical
31. "Dallas" family name
32. Boasts
33. Biochemistry abbr.
34. Cloy
35. Winged
36. Midday
37. Dadaism founder
38. Kind of group, in chemistry
39. Oscar winner for "The Cider House Rules"
40. Ruling
42. Talking points?
43. Quick sharp sound
44. 1968 British comedy "Only When I ___"
45. Sitting Bull, e.g.
47. Actress Rowlands
48. A person
51. Capital of Western Samoa
52. Dark purple bramble fruit
55. Tilt
56. Actress Virna
57. Solo
58. Work unit
59. Cornerstone abbr.
60. Seeped

DOWN

1. Extend across
2. ___ law
3. Small yeast cake
4. That, in Oaxaca
5. Relaxing
6. Strike breakers
7. Jekyll's alter ego
8. "Yo te ___"
9. Patrimony
10. Dance for three dancers
11. ___-Ball
12. Oceans
15. Coniferous evergreen forest
17. Suspicious (Colloq)
22. Butts
23. Sharpen
24. Muse of poetry
25. French equivalent of the Oscar
26. Conscious
27. Petty fault finding
28. Sturm und ___
29. Hole-___
30. Walking sticks
32. Close and open eyes quickly
35. Friendly
36. Naive person
38. Gray matter?: Abbr.
39. Water buffalo
41. Exult
42. Humid
44. Massenet opera
45. Fresh-water fish
46. On ___ with
47. Frighten
48. Josip ___ (Marshal Tito's original name)
49. Alencon's department
50. Changed colour of
53. Fleur-de-___
54. "Do Ya" rock grp.

ACROSS

1. Small rock
6. "Dilbert" intern
10. Chiang ___-shek
13. Carp
14. Painful
15. Window ledge
16. Nutritive
18. Bismarck's state: Abbr.
19. Carried out
20. Flashed signs
21. Backbones
23. Erode
24. Ancient city NW of Carthage
25. Aurochs
28. Slow cooker
31. Notions
32. "32 Flavors" singer Davis
33. In favour of
34. Subsided
35. Affect emotion
36. Vanquish
37. Codgers' replies
38. New wife
39. Lasses
40. Having no soul
42. Downy
43. Cries for attention
44. Pennant
45. Lilongwe is its capital
47. Prompted
48. Chatter
51. Galatea's love
52. Having nap almost worn off garment
55. ___ Strip
56. Actor Jannings
57. Reddish dye
58. Dutch city
59. Weeps
60. Of the nose

DOWN

1. Great quantity
2. Anklebones
3. Roman poet
4. Matchsticks game
5. Cricket teams
6. Flower
7. In order (to)
8. Bobby of hockey
9. Wedge-shaped stone at top of arch
10. Abductors
11. Wings: Lat.
12. Classes
15. Snip
17. Tidy
22. Size of type
23. Feeble
24. Salt of uric acid
25. Smartens (up)
26. State in the NW United States
27. Render sensual
28. Lumps of clay
29. Verbal exams
30. Hotsy-___
32. Wrong
35. Hermits
36. Bookstore sect.
38. Gusted
39. Make glad
41. Capital of Tibet
42. Parasitic insect
44. Coal, oil and petrol
45. Magician
46. Mil. school
47. Manger
48. Church service
49. Opera solo
50. Robt. E. Lee, e.g.
53. Med. care provider
54. Large snake

Puzzle 19

ACROSS
1. Kentucky college
6. Neighbor of Libya
10. Some batteries
13. Verbal exams
14. Mother of Apollo
15. Soyuz rocket letters
16. Tobacco holders
18. "___ way!"
19. Norse goddess
20. Turturro of "The Sopranos"
21. Cleaning ladies
23. Parentheses, e.g.
24. Mature
25. Turkish governors
28. Stately
31. These, in Madrid
32. Prefix with magnetic
33. Fleur-de-___
34. Inlets
35. Traditions
36. Diva ___ Te Kanawa
37. Buffalo's summer hrs.
38. Church walkway
39. "Socrate" composer
40. Pericarp
42. Of length
43. Salsa singer Cruz
44. Second letter of the Greek alphabet
45. Boeing rival
47. ___ de soie (silk cloth)
48. Star Wars, initially
51. Half court game?
52. Acted on one another
55. Heave
56. Never
57. Torment
58. Posed
59. Bloody
60. Bandleader Skinnay ___

DOWN
1. Nonsense
2. Sea eagle
3. Julia on screen
4. Fairy
5. Concerning
6. Lumps of clay
7. Prefix with -gon
8. Dined
9. Bundles of documents
10. Variety of amphibole
11. Molière play part
12. Healthful retreats
15. Military trainee
17. Popular pens
22. Lhasa ___
23. Triumphant cries
24. ___ show
25. Fathers
26. Stage whisper
27. Art of government
28. Blackbird
29. Its capital is Damascus
30. Willow
32. Cavity
35. Maintaining contact
36. Japanese syllabic script
38. Censorship-fighting org.
39. Locate
41. - and credit
42. "Laughable Lyrics" writer
44. Affected by beer
45. Exclamations of surprise
46. Intestinal parts
47. Wing: Prefix
48. 1972 Wimbledon winner Smith
49. Lucie's dad
50. Roman dates
53. Prefix, new
54. The 21st, e.g.: Abbr.

Puzzle 20

ACROSS

1. Assemblage of animals
6. Contaminate
11. Animation frame
14. Ancient Aegean land
15. Cartoon character, - Fudd
16. Bullfight call
17. Sparkle
19. Young louse
20. "Women and Love" author
21. Whinny
22. Final Four org.
23. Chinese dynasty
25. Weirdest
27. Arguers
31. Hindu music
32. Bank offering, for short
33. Muse of lyric poetry
35. Dame Nellie -
38. Explorer Cabeza de ___
40. Young salmon
42. Tears
43. Inquired
45. Daub
47. "___ won't be afraid" ("Stand by Me" lyric)
48. Larva
50. Rural plots of land
52. A Negro
55. Thoroughfare
56. Agave
57. Took examination again
59. Speaking platform
63. Monetary unit of Romania
64. Bright ideas
66. Cardinal number
67. Copy
68. Grunt
69. W.A. river
70. Football Hall-of-Famer Merlin
71. Old laborers

DOWN

1. Aquatic vertebrate
2. Positions
3. "I'm working ___!"
4. Movie theatre
5. "Krazy ___"
6. Telegraph messages
7. "___ want for Christmas ..."
8. Icon
9. Lower
10. Amount past due?
11. Hiding
12. Inventor Howe
13. Free to attack
18. Darts, bullseyes
22. African river
24. Manhattan addition
26. Male sheep
27. Prima donna
28. Periods of history
29. Opposed to foreground
30. Mouthlike opening
34. Upper end of the ulna
36. Fraternal org.
37. "No returns"
39. Eagle's nest
41. Fortune-telling cards (Pl)
44. French nobleman
46. "Bad Behavior" star, 1993
49. Tun
51. Extras
52. Finnish architect Alvar ___
53. Deride
54. Some tides
58. Father
60. "East of Eden" twin
61. Hungarian patriot Nagy
62. Fast fleet
64. "My man!"
65. "The Waste Land" monogram

40

Puzzle 21

ACROSS
1. Ursine animals
6. Theologian Kierkegaard
11. Cooking meas.
14. Enticed
15. Edict of the czar
16. Open
17. Creative ability
19. "The Crying Game" star
20. Lacquered metalware
21. Ex of the Donald
22. And others: Abbr.
23. Pain
25. People who las the distance
27. Infallible
31. Nobleman
32. Raincoat
33. Pertaining to the ileum
35. Sickened
38. Light: Prefix
40. Canadian physician Sir William ___
42. "___ kleine Nachtmusik"
43. Yemen's capital
45. Greek island
47. Beak
48. Former home to the Hawks, with "the"
50. Pleasure lover

52. Brassard
55. Hawaiian goose
56. Greek earth goddess: Var.
57. Jay Silverheels role
59. Affliction associated with rich foods
63. Like some stocks: Abbr.
64. A revival
66. Coastline feature
67. Boutros-Ghali's successor
68. Ever
69. "You've got mail" co.
70. Smarted
71. Of punishment

DOWN
1. Ink stain
2. Wallaroo
3. Husk
4. Change ratios of cogs
5. Star Wars, initially
6. Debonairness
7. Neighbor of Mo.
8. Precipitates
9. Worldly goods
10. Marshal at Waterloo
11. Trattoria treat
12. Lance
13. Bell ringings
18. Ex ___ (from

nothing)
22. Eagle's nest
24. ___ de coeur
26. Battery size
27. Ballpark figures
28. Okinawa port
29. Thrifty
30. Australian cockatoo
34. Concreting
36. Chemical endings
37. Something owing
39. Ballroom dance
41. Cowboy exhibitions
44. "___ Ng" (They Might Be Giants song)
46. Male child
49. Eager
51. Nullify
52. Ancient assembly area
53. Proportion
54. Italian lady
58. Indian bread
60. "Chestnuts roasting ___ open fire"
61. 1995 N.C.A.A. hoops champs
62. Inform
64. ___ Tafari (Haile Selassie)
65. Vital tree fluid

42

Puzzle 22

ACROSS
1. Odysseus, to the Cyclops Polyphemus
6. A tenth part
11. Nashville-based awards org.
14. Purgative injection
15. N.F.L. Hall-of-Famer Hirsch
16. Intention
17. Negotiate again
19. 22.5 degrees
20. Thrash
21. Plait
22. Knowing, as a secret
23. Seat of Allen County, Kan.
25. Construction site machines
27. Conveyance by trucks
31. Sea bird
32. Howard of "Happy Days"
33. Courtyards
35. Icy
38. A particular
40. Keen
42. Cupola
43. Silent actor
45. Lakes
47. Decryption org.
48. Prepare patient for operation
50. The turning on an axis
52. Can opener
55. Broad-topped hill, in the Southwest
56. Blackthorn
57. Ventilate again
59. Upswept hairdo
63. Some
64. The Archer
66. New Guinea seaport
67. Worship
68. Ice hockey balls
69. ___ school
70. "For ___ sake!"
71. Bone: Prefix

DOWN
1. Dweeb
2. Unique thing
3. List of dishes
4. Protozoan
5. Henpeck
6. Word of four letters
7. Hip bones
8. Path
9. Frankfurter
10. Optic organ
11. Tubular pasta
12. Underaged person
13. Words of agreement
18. Flattened at the poles
22. Lazed
24. River to the Volga
26. Calendar abbr.
27. Decorate (Xmas tree)
28. French roast
29. Without a job
30. Swiss mountain
34. Meteors
36. "___ Excited" (Pointer Sisters hit)
37. University head
39. Blackbird
41. Reply
44. Soak
46. Uncle -, USA personified
49. Procession
51. Star sign
52. Sacred song
53. Arm bones
54. Procreated
58. Frigid finish
60. Cropped photos?
61. Nobleman
62. ___ buco
64. Plant juice
65. G.I.'s mail drop

ACROSS
1. Marine hazards
6. Walk
11. Düsseldorf direction
14. Castilian hero
15. Full of hills
16. 1959 hit with a melody based on the folk song "The Wreck of the Old 97"
17. Qualification document
19. Arrest
20. Tense
21. Salt of uric acid
22. Lover of Aeneas
23. Founded: Abbr.
25. Automaker Maserati
27. An opening
31. 1960's civil rights org.
32. Kid's cry
33. European mountains
35. Squeezing (out)
38. Ova
40. Bothered
42. Prophet
43. Memento
45. Invest
47. Not
48. Egress
50. With skill
52. Coming up
55. Hydrocarbon suffixes
56. Risque
57. Vapid
59. Inlets
63. ___, amas, amat …
64. The act of forbidding
66. Modern: Ger.
67. Decorate
68. Tests by lifting
69. Believer's suffix
70. Baseball exec Bud
71. Astringent fruit

DOWN
1. Prefix with angular
2. Zeno of ___
3. Colour of unbleached linen
4. Tailor, at times
5. Cold war abbr.
6. Lousy
7. Costa ___
8. Overjoy
9. Changes
10. Change colour of
11. Having unlimited knowledge
12. German town
13. Forbidden
18. Old Ford model
22. Ship's floors
24. "Rugrats" dad
26. Austin-to-Dallas dir.
27. Certain league: Abbr.
28. Book leaf
29. Highest rank in scouting
30. "Uncle Vanya" woman
34. Making morose
36. "Hud" Oscar winner
37. Hoar
39. Threescore
41. Revolved
44. A.F.L.'s partner
46. Help wanted abbr.
49. Electrical rectifier with three electrodes
51. Republic in SW Asia
52. Khomeini, for one
53. Titles
54. Sign up
58. Dugout shelter
60. Information
61. Entr'___
62. Cong. period
64. Scale notes
65. Some batters, for short

Puzzle 24

ACROSS

1. Below
6. Conscript
11. U.S. Army medal
14. Moslem religion
15. More mature
16. Questioning exclamation
17. Temporariness
19. "Aladdin" prince
20. As soon as possible
21. Applause
22. "___ Lang Syne"
23. Therefore
25. Celestial clouds
27. Snood
31. Wrinkle
32. Short trader?
33. ___ artery
35. Murder victim Kanka with a law named after her
38. Gds.
40. Noblemen
42. Travel on
43. Woodland deity
45. Female relative
47. Confederate soldier, for short
48. Redact
50. Planetariums
52. Amusing
55. Hereditary factor
56. Tennis star, - Natase
57. Skater Harding
59. Promontory
63. Kangaroo
64. Suggested strongly
66. French vineyard
67. Smell
68. Jiltee of myth
69. Masthead contents, briefly
70. Big Bertha's birthplace
71. Smelled foul

DOWN

1. Actress Talbot
2. Go-aheads
3. "Summer and Smoke" heroine
4. Knocked lightly
5. Med. plan
6. Harsh, rigorous
7. Rivulet
8. Of bees
9. Manacle
10. Attempt
11. A peak of the Himalayas
12. Roman general
13. Reprimand
18. Entertain
22. Tool for boring holes
24. Baseball card stat.
26. Hobo
27. Overacts
28. "Das Rheingold" goddess
29. Temperate
30. Italian playwright ___ Fo
34. Minister of a church
36. "Song of the South" song syllables
37. Beaks
39. Singer Gorme
41. Yell
44. Rocker Ocasek
46. Even (poet.)
49. Spuds
51. Milk curdler
52. "Odyssey" enchantress
53. "What now?!"
54. Train engines
58. Iditarod terminus
60. Mythology anthology
61. Observed
62. Badlands Natl. Park locale
64. "Norma ___"
65. Printer's measures

Puzzle 25

ACROSS

1. Inflicts pain
6. ___ diem
11. "The ___ Daba Honeymoon"
14. Large body of water
15. Fake fat brand
16. Gear wheel
17. Visible to the naked eye
19. "Anderson Cooper 360°" channel
20. One's parents (Colloq)
21. Something that consumes
22. First-class
23. Years abroad
25. Associations
27. Wealthy
31. "Whatcha ___?"
32. Hive insect
33. More gelid
35. Relatively cool sun
38. Bric-a-___
40. Indian of Mexico
42. Story
43. Con men?
45. Rub out
47. Takeaway game
48. Meeting centre
50. Some Ghana natives
52. Axiom
55. Hindu garment
56. Prohibits
57. Conductor Kurt
59. Lotto-like gambling game
63. Gambling inits.
64. Ventures
66. Prefix, new
67. ___ Dame
68. In any way
69. Author LeShan
70. Donkeys
71. Saint in Brazil

DOWN

1. - sapiens, Man
2. West Coast sch.
3. In-basket stamp: Abbr.
4. Of the ankle
5. ___-Caps
6. Affect by cocaine
7. "Thanks ___!"
8. Drive back
9. Coupled
10. Abbr. at the bottom of a letter
11. Person skilled in accounting
12. "___ chance!"
13. Moorehead of "Bewitched"
18. American Indian tribe
22. Pay for grazing
24. Rapa ___ (Easter Island)
26. Very good (1-2)
27. Swedish pop-group of the '70s
28. Fronded plant
29. It's a wrap
30. Prefix, four
34. Gives hope to
36. Others, in Latin
37. Radiation dosages
39. Slangy greetings
41. Black key
44. Camera type, briefly
46. Otic organ
49. Greek island
51. Premier Khrushchev
52. Choice steak (1-4)
53. Loathed
54. Slugger Williams and others
58. Withered
60. Son of Isaac and Rebekah
61. "Little" Dickens girl
62. Capital of Norway
64. Bambi's aunt
65. Knock vigorously

Puzzle 26

ACROSS
1. Aches
6. Indian melodies
11. Throw lightly
14. ___ time
15. ___ ware (Japanese porcelain)
16. Dined
17. Haphazard
19. Bull's-eye: Abbr.
20. "Do the Right Thing" pizzeria
21. Clay pigeon
22. Great age
23. U.S. TV award
25. Nonpile cotton rug of India
27. Made by hand
31. Epithet of Athena
32. Malt beverage
33. "All My Children" vixen
35. Garden flower
38. Portent
40. Battery terminal
42. Josip Broz, familiarly
43. Prefix, sun
45. Bright arc light
47. ___ power
48. Arctic native
50. United
52. Ladies' men
55. High, clear ringing sound
56. Level

57. Louvre, par exemple
59. Ireland
63. Grandmother
64. Incidents
66. Abbr. in a business letter
67. Zoroastrian
68. Plenty
69. - kwon do (Korean martial art)
70. Water vapour
71. Old "Hollywood Squares" regular

DOWN
1. Name of 12 popes
2. Indian currency
3. Object of worship
4. Nurtured
5. Line part: Abbr.
6. Small-time
7. Friend, to Françoise
8. Stared
9. "___ Sings the Blues" (1980 album)
10. Half-brother of Tom Sawyer
11. Tearing
12. 10th-century Holy Roman emperor
13. Swiss capital
18. Capital of Eritrea
22. "Give it ___!"

24. Abbr. on a French envelope
26. Suffix with form
27. Jumble
28. "That's ___!"
29. Failure to take due care
30. Bacteria discovered by Theodor Escherich
34. In the meantime
36. "___, Brute!"
37. Architect Mies van der ___
39. Curtain fabric
41. Harder to grasp
44. Lubricant
46. Information
49. Male cat
51. Bureau
52. "The Maids" playwright
53. Ex-Mrs. Trump
54. Monetary unit of Ecuador
58. Ruined city in W Iran
60. Words of confidence
61. Spawning area of salmon
62. Sum, ___, fui
64. Operations (colloq)
65. Immigrant's class: Abbr.

Puzzle 27

ACROSS

1. Destined
6. Agave fibre
11. Fraternity letters
14. Monetary unit of Sierra Leone
15. Television repeat
16. Can. province
17. Extirpating
19. "Trust ___" (1937 hit)
20. Be foolishly fond of
21. 1970 World's Fair site
22. Young horse
23. Part of the Bible: Abbr.
25. Saint-___ (Loire's capital)
27. Edible turtle
31. New newts
32. Arthur Godfrey played it
33. Pertaining to a tube
35. Composer Saint-___
38. Units of loudness
40. Worked at
42. Old knife
43. Skilled
45. Poland Spring competitor
47. Title of a knight
48. Hindu teacher
50. Greedy
52. Readjust
55. Donald Duck, to his nephews
56. Non-scientific studies
57. Core
59. Forbidden: Var.
63. Magician's name ending
64. Earthly
66. Author ___ Yutang
67. Synthetic fabric
68. Actor Quinn
69. Part: Abbr.
70. Untidy
71. Seat of Marion County, Fla.

DOWN

1. Ran from
2. Prefix, air
3. Just right
4. Make beloved
5. "Agnus ___"
6. Easily angered
7. Bristle
8. Early wheels
9. Shaped like a crescent
10. Chang's Siamese twin
11. Practical or strict attitude (2-8)
12. Deprive of courage
13. Commemorative marker
18. Confine
22. Brine-cured cheeses
24. Dab
26. Possibilities
27. Wind instrument
28. Barely managed, with "out"
29. Banishing
30. Artless
34. Without haste
36. Düsseldorf denial
37. Muralist José María ___
39. Taters
41. Frightens
44. "La la" preceder
46. A.E.C. successor
49. "Yoo-hoo!"
51. Medical
52. Train tracks
53. "It's a Wonderful Life" role
54. Sea birds
58. Greek god of war
60. "O patria mia" singer
61. False god
62. Arm bone
64. Scottish cap
65. Chinese "way"

Puzzle 28

ACROSS
1. Snares
6. Minor oath
11. Cable alternative
14. Containing iodine
15. Naked pictures
16. Nasdaq debut: Abbr.
17. Sustenance
19. "The Raven" author
20. Seaward
21. Spanish houses
22. Brit. decorations
23. "Fargo" director
25. Sores
27. Temporary inactivity
31. Quantity of paper
32. O.A.S. member: Abbr.
33. Clinton cabinet member
35. South American ruminant
38. "Li'l Abner" cartoonist
40. Hair net
42. Cosy
43. Gravestone
45. Pasted
47. Expert finish
48. U.S. space agency
50. Supply with water

52. Tar
55. Greek goddess of the earth
56. Meaningless chatter
57. Diplomat Boutros Boutros-___
59. Fitness centers
63. Poke
64. Making normal
66. Big picture?: Abbr.
67. Nabisco cookies
68. Foreign assembly
69. Pedal digit
70. Sideshow performers
71. "Awake and Sing!" playwright

DOWN
1. She played Ginger on "Gilligan's Island"
2. Little hoppers
3. Together, in music
4. Robbery at sea
5. Biol., e.g.
6. Embellishing
7. Mouth parts
8. "Let's Make ___"
9. Thicker
10. Atl. crosser
11. Irresistible craving for alcohol

12. Eating utensil
13. Loam deposit
18. Vistas
22. Faces
24. Lever for rowing
26. Partner of poivre
27. Gremlins, Pacers, etc.
28. Strike forcefully
29. Capable of being done without
30. Dangerous bacteria
34. Sandglass
36. Mould
37. "A Death in the Family" author
39. Gentle splash
41. Run off tracks
44. Gray of "Gray's Manual of Botany"
46. Expire
49. "Earth in the Balance" author
51. Gossiped
52. ___ d'art
53. Grassy plain
54. Triad
58. Crazily
60. Languish
61. Gray's subj.
62. Certain NCO's
64. Egg drink
65. Equal: Prefix

Puzzle 29

ACROSS

1. Stringed instruments
6. Explosive sounds
11. Took a seat
14. "As You Like It" setting
15. Sorbonne, e.g.
16. Chop
17. Not catalectic
19. Nothing
20. Frighten
21. Regularly
22. A Turner
23. Article for Mozart
25. Parts tuned on a violin
27. Cotyledon
31. Chair
32. Tavern
33. "The Sopranos" restaurateur
35. Scorning persons
38. Cabinet dept.
40. Organization
42. Midge
43. Style
45. Puerto ___
47. Wrath
48. Roulette bet
50. Turnip-shaped
52. Under debate
55. Mother of Apollo
56. Bath requisite
57. From Nineveh: Abbr.
59. Singular, to Caesar
63. Take a seat
64. Preventing fever
66. Beer
67. Spy
68. Pointed arch
69. My, French (Plural)
70. Antlers
71. Heavy drinker

DOWN

1. Dutch name of The Hague
2. Medieval chest
3. Nutritional info
4. Caressed
5. Simple fastener
6. Yeoman of the guard
7. Billing abbr.
8. Memoranda
9. Gleams
10. Dry (wine)
11. Site of the Alamo
12. Firing
13. U.S. State. Capital Austin
18. Ones who dislike company
22. Chinese unit of weight
24. Dockworkers' org.
26. ___ gestae
27. Victory: Ger.
28. "Momo" author Michael
29. Pronounces in a specific manner
30. Belong
34. Australian trees
36. "Roseanne" star
37. Stalk
39. Brittle
41. Like paper
44. Abstract being
46. Young louse
49. Autonomous government organization
51. Precede
52. State in NE India
53. Fine linen
54. Chemical compound
58. ___ Fein
60. On one's toes
61. Split
62. The maple
64. Exclamation of surprise
65. Decay

Puzzle 30

ACROSS
1. Strike breaker
5. French assembly
10. Punnily titled 1952 quiz show "Up to ___"
14. Cougar
15. Dennis the Menace's mother
16. They, in Trieste
17. Wanes
18. Alcove
19. Cube
20. Fragrant flowers
22. Famous escapologist, Harry -
24. Immune response orchestrator
25. Subject of discussion
26. Brass wind instrument
29. Weight measure
33. Dog's warning
36. Reef of coral
40. Uproar
42. Greg Evans comic strip
43. The Orient
44. Levees
47. Ltr. addenda
48. Garrulous
49. Eastern titles
51. Slow

55. Ostrich-like birds
59. Woman who writes poetry
61. Spurious
62. Chrysalis
63. Big name in kitchen foil
65. In a bad way
66. German Mrs
67. Drink to
68. "Star Wars" princess
69. Ashy substance
70. Noted Detroit brewer
71. Wall St. figures

DOWN
1. Read out letters of a word
2. Having the form of a cube
3. Stroll
4. Igneous rock of a lava flow
5. Without
6. Biblical high priest
7. Not, in Nuremberg
8. Allergy season sound
9. Get ready to drive
10. Care of the feet
11. "Q ___ queen"
12. Fungal spore sacs
13. Female ruff

21. Cudgel
23. Christian name
27. Shy
28. Jack-in-the-pulpit, e.g.
30. Lowest high tide
31. British tax
32. Newts
33. Diver Louganis
34. Terza ___ (Italian verse form)
35. All-Star reliever Nen
37. "The Facts of Life" actress
38. Taverns
39. ___'acte
41. Pageants
45. Russian no
46. Knights' titles
50. Young woman
52. ___-foot oil
53. Letter-shaped opening
54. Academy Award
56. Noted blind mathematician
57. Improvise (speech)
58. Nutritious beans
59. Aqua ___
60. Iridescent gem
61. Walkway
62. Army E-3
64. Spanish bear

Puzzle 31

ACROSS
1. ___ Grande, Fla.
5. Breezing through
10. Part of a nuclear arsenal, for short
14. 1953 Leslie Caron film
15. Malay island
16. Temple
17. Airline to Israel
18. Funny Anne
19. Helsinki citizen
20. Eagles' nests
22. Affectedly dainty
24. Basic monetary unit of Sweden
25. Glossy fabric
26. Understand
29. Assistants
33. Gen.'s counterpart
36. Possessing full power
40. Bubbly name
42. Woman with ___
43. Counting-out bit
44. Stingy
47. Ed.'s request
48. Flight of steps
49. Hindu titles
51. Asian country
55. Sofia's portrayer in "The Color Purple"

59. Arrangement of several pictures into one
61. Breakwater
62. Drill
63. Truss
65. As previously given
66. Applies friction to
67. Prefers
68. Champagne Tony of golf
69. Pause
70. Beginning
71. 1982 Disney film

DOWN
1. Desolate
2. Oilcan
3. Humidor item
4. Sickening
5. Bill producers
6. Inc., overseas
7. Mosque officials
8. Water wheel
9. Concede
10. Boundless
11. First son of Adam and Eve
12. Dull resonant sound
13. AOL alternative
21. Wyatt -
23. Goodbye

27. Elgar's "King ___"
28. French military cap
30. Barely passing grades
31. Sicilian city
32. Eye inflammation
33. Nos. on checks
34. "Go ahead!"
35. Prefix, large
37. "If I Ruled the World" rapper
38. Adherents
39. Wing: Prefix
41. Leanest
45. Weight allowance
46. Last name in fashion
50. Gone bad
52. Artist Picasso
53. Smiling
54. Loses water
56. Actress Winona
57. Prefix, wind
58. Virile male
59. Pout
60. Eyes, poetically
61. Romance tale
62. "Can we move this inside?"
64. Big section in a dictionary

Puzzle 32

ACROSS

1. Public swimming pool
5. Moisten meat while cooking
10. Religious title: Abbr.
14. Bolt holder
15. Pains
16. "Moby Dick" captain
17. Young horse
18. Bedding item
19. Follower of Hitler
20. Beginnings
22. Burning up
24. Ogles
25. Capital of Afghanistan
26. Car from Trollhättan
29. Finds shelter
33. TV's "Emerald Point ___"
36. Hotel amenity
40. Drug-yielding plant
42. Obsequious act
43. Greek god of love
44. Containing caffeine
47. Abstract being
48. Flips (through)
49. City on the Oka
51. Articles
55. Author Zora ___ Hurston
59. Republic in W Africa
61. Person of experience
62. First name in 50's TV
63. ___ show
65. Extinct bird
66. Together, musically
67. Greek letter
68. Auspices
69. Dosage amts.
70. Rest atop
71. Finished

DOWN

1. Maj.'s superior
2. Combined
3. Edible red seaweed
4. Marine mammals
5. Low in pitch
6. "___ du lieber!"
7. Arab chief
8. "Lovergirl" singer ___ Marie
9. Cornerstone abbr.
10. "Holy smokes!"
11. Cormorant
12. Stare
13. Baseball stat
21. Russian emperor
23. Essen basin
27. Golfer Isao
28. Benefit
30. Dreadful
31. Coll. major
32. Legis. meeting
33. Table salt, to a chemist
34. Wings
35. Couch
37. 1959 Kingston Trio hit
38. "And ___ bed"
39. Pitcher
41. Images
45. Punta del ___, Uruguay
46. Dint
50. Containing tetraethyllead
52. Cedric ___ of "Little Lord Fauntleroy"
53. Algonquian tribe member
54. Eastern wrap
56. As much as you like
57. Ushered
58. Uneven
59. Beatty and Rorem
60. "The jig ___!"
61. - Connery
62. "Can't Help Lovin' ___ Man"
64. The self

ACROSS
1. "Santa Baby" singer
5. Source of cocoa
10. Den
14. A Great Lake
15. Convex molding
16. Yorkshire river
17. Afflicts
18. Coniferous tree
19. Lyrical
20. Sleeping sickness fly
22. Soft leather
24. Tatter
25. Hindu ascetic
26. Baby's first word
29. Lyric poem
33. Pig
36. Kcal
40. Big furniture retailer
42. Illinois city
43. Notch
44. Conversion
47. Some appliances
48. Of Salian Franks
49. Seagoing: Abbr.
51. Cane product
55. Pope's cape
59. Dark syrup

61. Sleeping noises
62. Deride
63. Hanging limply
65. Subatomic particle
66. Others, to Octavian
67. Early computer
68. Corn ___
69. For fear that
70. Yard enclosure
71. Elevator inventor

DOWN
1. English poet
2. Erse
3. Roofer
4. Tried
5. "Unforgettable" singer
6. Clark's "Mogambo" co-star
7. Thin ropes
8. Major can maker
9. ___ and aahed
10. Regard
11. Autobahn auto
12. "Beauty ___ the eye ..."
13. ___ room
21. Minn. neighbor
23. Author Silverstein
27. Clock face

28. Friend
30. At first: Abbr.
31. Gaming cubes
32. Fun house sounds
33. Coxae
34. Creole vegetable
35. Earth sci.
37. His "4" was retired
38. Piece of money
39. Looped handle
41. Opinion opener
45. O.A.S. member: Abbr.
46. Unstable lepton
50. Deranged from tropical heat (Colloq)
52. Staff leader?
53. Isolated
54. Adjust, as a brooch
56. Running wild
57. Actress Téa
58. Old laborers
59. Roofing slate
60. Aaron's 2,297
61. Stable attendant
62. Girl (Slang)
64. ___-Man (arcade game)

Puzzle 33

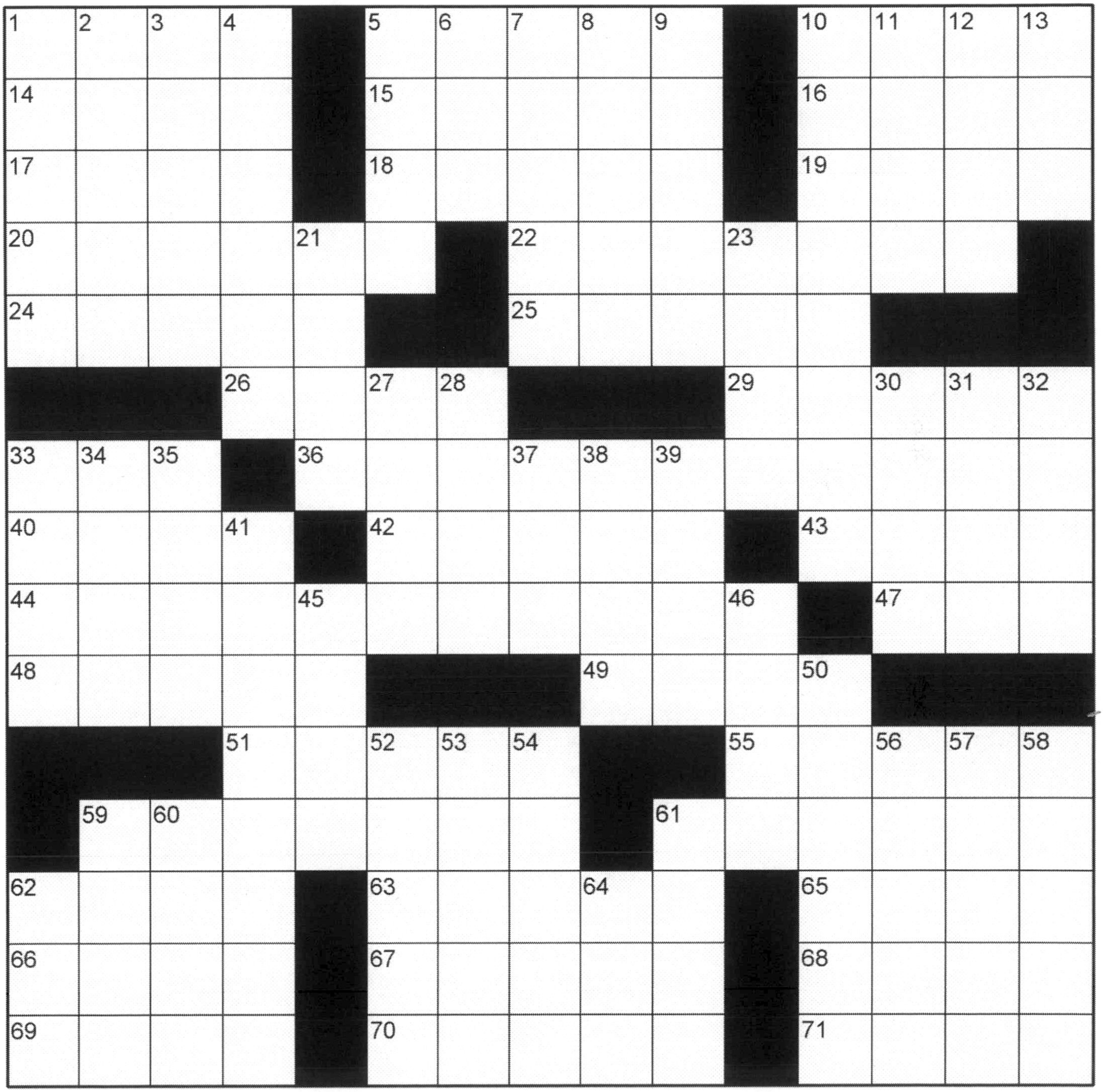
1 2 3 4 5 6 7 8 9 10 11 12 13
14 15 16
17 18 19
20 21 22 23
24 25
26 27 28 29 30 31 32
33 34 35 36 37 38 39
40 41 42 43
44 45 46 47
48 49 50
51 52 53 54 55 56 57 58
59 60 61
62 63 64 65
66 67 68
69 70 71

Puzzle 34

ACROSS

1. Eastern nurse
5. Wash
10. Fishing reel
14. "Come Back, Little Sheba" wife
15. Body of salt water
16. The maple
17. Vow
18. Helping theorem
19. 1988 country album
20. Threaten
22. Mollycoddles
24. Black Sea port, new-style
25. First name in 2000 news
26. Bob Hoskins's role in "Hook"
29. Anatomical canals
33. Republicans, for short
36. Overstated
40. Asia's Trans ___ mountains
42. Item having exchange value
43. A Turner
44. Legal offense
47. "Mighty ___ a Rose"
48. Red dye
49. Soon
51. Greek theatre
55. Ancient region in S Mesopotamia
59. Shaped like a hood
61. Texas/Louisiana border river
62. Fresh-water fish
63. Respond
65. "Casablanca" heroine
66. University mil. group
67. Went wrong
68. Praise
69. Narrow opening
70. Measures of medicine
71. Chemical endings

DOWN

1. A poplar
2. Budged
3. Coeur d'___, Idaho
4. Torment
5. Tree trunk
6. Top card
7. Fiesta Bowl site
8. Porter
9. As a friend, to François
10. Of parents
11. "Happy Birthday" writer
12. Civil War side
13. "We Do Our Part" org.
21. Arrived
23. Duo
27. Test
28. Relax
30. Bibliog. space saver
31. Actress Sofer
32. Neb. neighbor
33. Brave
34. Potpourri
35. Succeed in examination
37. Fed. construction overseer
38. Actress Rowlands
39. English college
41. Person's individual speech pattern
45. "Momo" author Michael
46. Santa ___, Calif.
50. Marriageable
52. Having ears
53. Alamogordo's county
54. Draws close to
56. Where to see "The Last Supper"
57. Result
58. Peruses
59. Jail
60. Part of a Spanish play
61. Benchmarks: Abbr.
62. A.M.A. members
64. Canadian capital?

Puzzle 35

ACROSS
1. Toboggan
5. Philosopher William of ___
10. Large almost tailless rodent
14. Jekyll's counterpart
15. Dirt
16. Norse god
17. Beaten by tennis service
18. Singer Lopez
19. Anchovy containers
20. Madagascan mammals
22. Family name
24. Percolate
25. Braid
26. A dog's age
29. King with golden touch
33. ___ Kan
36. Rustic garden
40. Frozen confections
42. "It ain't over till it's over" speaker
43. Turner and others
44. "Jeopardy!" phrase
47. "___ Boot"
48. Hawk's nest
49. Scorning person
51. Shoestrings
55. Person born under the sign of the Ram
59. Ochlocracy
61. Thin
62. Titicaca, por ejemplo
63. Fab Four member
65. Actress Merrill
66. "The Snowy Day" author ___ Jack Keats
67. Doughnut-shaped roll
68. "___ in Calico" (1946 song)
69. Root vegetable
70. Fits of rage
71. "Damn Yankees" seductress

DOWN
1. Will
2. Certain école
3. Dropsy
4. Infer
5. Chooses
6. Minced oath
7. Brittle
8. Invalidate
9. Actress Kelly
10. Act of drinking
11. Take ___ view of
12. Motion picture
13. Years, to Yves
21. Frat letters
23. "The Secret of ___" (1982 film)
27. Central parts
28. Old World duck
30. Couple
31. "The Thin Man" pooch
32. Meeting: Abbr.
33. Bird of prey
34. Having aches
35. Ogle
37. G.I. chow in Desert Storm
38. Blows it
39. Precipitation
41. Boat having sails
45. Close
46. Saturate
50. For a bride
52. Restrains
53. Name in 2000 headlines
54. Monetary unit of Zaire
56. Architect Jones
57. Chronicle
58. African antelope
59. Labyrinth
60. Monster
61. Musical notes
62. Isr. neighbor
64. Obtain

Puzzle 36

ACROSS
1. Visage
5. "The Gondoliers" girl
10. Entrance
14. Hydrocarbon suffixes
15. Epileptic seizure
16. Merit
17. Auspices: Var.
18. Shore
19. Ostrich-like bird
20. Defames
22. Metallic element of the platinum family
24. Combs et al.
25. Bolshoi rival
26. Every
29. Assembly rooms
33. Exclamation of surprise
36. Something converted from one language to another
40. Cast aside
42. Japanese dog
43. To be, in old Rome
44. Arrange in alphabetical order
47. Consumed
48. 1953 A.L. M.V.P.
49. Bakery selections
51. Indian currency
55. Frosted
59. Small bouquet
61. Map line joining equal barometric pressures
62. Narcotics agent
63. Extinct birds
65. "Thank Heaven for Little Girls" musical
66. Egyptian deity
67. Lifeless
68. "Zip-___-Doo-Dah"
69. Depend
70. Actor Lew
71. Composer Rorem and others

DOWN
1. Touches
2. 1973 #1 Rolling Stones hit
3. Silk cotton
4. Jewish fraternity
5. Quirks
6. "A Theory of Semiotics" author
7. Unadorned
8. Japanese dish
9. Mary of "The Maltese Falcon"
10. Something derived
11. Island of Hawaii
12. City just south of Timpanogos Cave National Monument
13. Biology class abbr.
21. Aspiring atty.'s exam
23. Qatar's capital
27. Crustacean
28. Codlike fish
30. "Mona ___"
31. Was defeated
32. Old-fashioned knife
33. Slightly open
34. Hawaii County's seat
35. Peaks
37. Louse egg
38. Agitate
39. Slothful
41. System of deities
45. Landers and others
46. Lines of thought, for short?
50. Catchword
52. Bela coached her in 1976
53. Severe pain
54. Exodus commemoration
56. Live
57. Behind bars
58. Enemies of the Iroquois
59. Blanchett of "Elizabeth"
60. Spoken
61. Believers
62. "All Things Considered" airer
64. Crude mineral

Puzzle 37

ACROSS
1. The villain in Othello
5. Mediterranean island
10. Sandy tract
14. Sound of a cat
15. A Musketeer
16. Apple product
17. Elvis ___ Presley
18. Clever
19. Breathe with relief
20. Tight-fisted people
22. Hot wind
24. Prophets
25. Garlic-flavored mayonnaise
26. Cinematographer Nykvist
29. Fencing equipment
33. N.Y.C. subway
36. Study of the planets
40. Raccoon
42. Province of Spain
43. "The Dukes of Hazzard" spinoff
44. Theme of this puzzle
47. Boom source
48. Snake
49. ___ prof.
51. Hipbone-related
55. Covered with ceramic pieces
59. Seaport in SW Italy
61. "Later!"
62. Against
63. Actress Taylor of "The Nanny"
65. Understand
66. "Norma Rae" director
67. Antelope
68. Acquire through merit
69. Tiny, informally
70. Hereditary factors
71. Brinks

DOWN
1. Mosque priests
2. Lofty nest
3. Large duck-like bird
4. Proprietors
5. Aggregate
6. Store convenience, for short
7. Capital of Tibet
8. Japanese gateway
9. Nolan Ryan, notably
10. Apostle
11. Heroic
12. Canceled
13. Old English letter
21. Common request
23. Blue Bonnet, e.g.
27. Airline to Tel Aviv
28. Marine defence unit
30. Ages and ages
31. Personalities
32. Method: Abbr.
33. SALT concern
34. "A Doll's House" heroine
35. Fate
37. A fool
38. Zeno's home
39. Soviet news service
41. Those of high birth
45. Cabbagelike plant
46. "Como ___ usted?"
50. Mender of pots and pans
52. Like some vbs.
53. Anoint
54. ___ the Barbarian
56. Hawaiian island
57. Huge
58. Sunrises
59. Fit of rage
60. Lawyers: Abbr.
61. Club ___ (resorts)
62. "Exodus" character
64. Chemical ending

74

Puzzle 38

ACROSS
1. Tach readings
5. "Waterworld" girl
10. Restrain
14. Sundae topper, perhaps
15. Like a shoe
16. Wallaroo
17. Officiating priest of a mosque
18. Subject to the ocean's movements
19. Bothers
20. City on the Rio Grande
22. Disgruntled
24. Trap
25. Granddaddy of all computers
26. Sledge
29. One of the United Arab Emirates
33. "Nova" network
36. Arranged alphabetically
40. Intestinal parts
42. Two islands in the N Bahamas
43. Notes at scale's ends
44. High-minded
47. Clock std.
48. Japanese beer brand
49. Kraft Nabisco Championship org.
51. Celts and Gaels
55. Coronet
59. Squash
61. Dormant
62. Greek consonants
63. TV's "The George & ___ Show"
65. Munich's river
66. "Dies ___"
67. Rubbernecker
68. "In the Still of the ___" (Boyz II Men hit)
69. Two identical things
70. Precipitous
71. Mardi ___

DOWN
1. Vexes
2. Spin doctor
3. Half a comedy duo
4. "Three's Company" actress
5. "___ Perpetua" (Idaho's motto)
6. "___ won't!"
7. A parent
8. Rimes of country music
9. 1950's candidate Stevenson
10. Tofu
11. Autobahn sight
12. Canter
13. Greek goddess of the dawn
21. Boxing's Oscar ___ Hoya
23. Thompson of "Family"
27. Abba of Israel
28. Actress Mazar
30. Bookstore sect.
31. Exclamations of surprise
32. Current month
33. Cotton fabric
34. "Gil ___"
35. Big name in computer games
37. Eccentric wheel
38. E.P.A. concern: Abbr.
39. Arrange, as hair
41. Big name in brewing
45. Leeds's river
46. Some N.C.O.'s
50. Sick
52. Metal drosses
53. Showy actions
54. Mould
56. Race of Norse gods
57. Gaucho's rope
58. ___-ski
59. "Nobody doesn't like ___ Lee"
60. Paris's ___ d'Orsay
61. Modern Maturity grp.
62. Gratuity
64. Born

Puzzle 39

ACROSS
1. Repair
5. Cleft in two
10. Cooperstown nickname
14. "Dragonwyck" author Seton
15. Gland: Prefix
16. River in central Switzerland
17. Benedictine monks' titles
18. Female servants
19. Much may follow it
20. Top dogs
22. Mischievous sprite
24. "Politically Incorrect" host
25. Lowest point
26. Ritual
29. Civil rights org.
33. Chest bone
36. Expert in logistics
40. Seat of Allen County, Kansas
42. Microwave emitter
43. Sea eagle
44. Conceit
47. French, water
48. Language spoken in S China
49. Group of two
51. Perfume with incense
55. Astronomer Tycho
59. Exploit
61. Stage whispers
62. Anchor vessel
63. Man of many words?
65. Old cloth measures
66. Short tail
67. New Mexico county
68. Ward of "Once and Again"
69. ___-Ball (arcade game)
70. Lug
71. Ilium

DOWN
1. Feminine address
2. ___ Gay
3. Beautiful maiden
4. Plunger for churning butter
5. Loud hits
6. Highest mountain in Crete
7. Pretend
8. Chief of the Vedic gods
9. Administered medicine to
10. Channel leading away
11. Indian queen
12. Republic in SW Asia
13. French possessive
21. Seed coat
23. Short dress
27. Large volume
28. Minor oath
30. Suffix with concession
31. Scene of first miracle
32. French tire
33. Endanger
34. U.S. State
35. Lost blood
37. Book end?
38. Pip
39. Salver
41. Menu option
45. Prevaricated
46. Applies lightly
50. Most parched
52. ___ Circus (where St. Peter was crucified)
53. Truth (Archaic)
54. TV actress Georgia
56. Freud contemporary
57. A greeting
58. Short story
59. Clock sound
60. Don Juan, e.g.
61. At the apex
62. Ed.'s in-box filler
64. Before

Puzzle 40

ACROSS

1. Fairytale
6. Bridge declaration
11. Plaintive cry
14. Young owl
15. Stair post
16. Software program, briefly
17. Precedence
19. ___ Pensacola (mil. center)
20. Ed.'s pile
21. Tress
22. Period of office
24. Repeated, singer who sang with Cult Jam
25. Manages
26. Depart
29. Fierce
32. Set up again
33. Water-repellent cloth
34. Thor Heyerdahl craft
35. Chrysler Building architect William Van ___
36. Melon
37. Coat with gold
38. Beer barrel
39. Plinth
40. Tree
41. Devouring
43. Person in debt
44. Skins
45. Adds
46. Vail trail
48. Silent
49. "___ nuff!"
52. Dove's call
53. Streamlined
56. "Aladdin" monkey
57. Russian emperors
58. Veracity
59. "Der Ring ___ Nibelungen"
60. Short literary composition
61. "Bellefleur" author

DOWN

1. Froth
2. Barley beards
3. Diner orders
4. Shelter
5. Engraving with acid
6. Asian nation
7. Noble
8. Grain beard
9. Divided into sectors
10. Think about
11. Hand written document
12. On ___ with (equal to)
13. Church recess
18. Relaxation
23. Opposite of alt
24. Meat cut
25. Key personnel
26. Arrest car's movement
27. Sniggled
28. Sociable
29. Infringements of rules in sports
30. Shout of exultation
31. Duck with soft down
33. Locality
36. Virtue
37. Goes on and on
39. Sinuous
40. Souvenir
42. Geom. figure
43. Obligation
45. Resembling suds
46. Great quantity
47. 1995 earthquake site
48. Atlanta Falcons head coach Jim
49. Filth
50. Sexologist Shere
51. Big name in newspaper publishing
54. Dorm authority figures: Abbr.
55. ___-A (drug used to treat chickenpox)

Puzzle 40

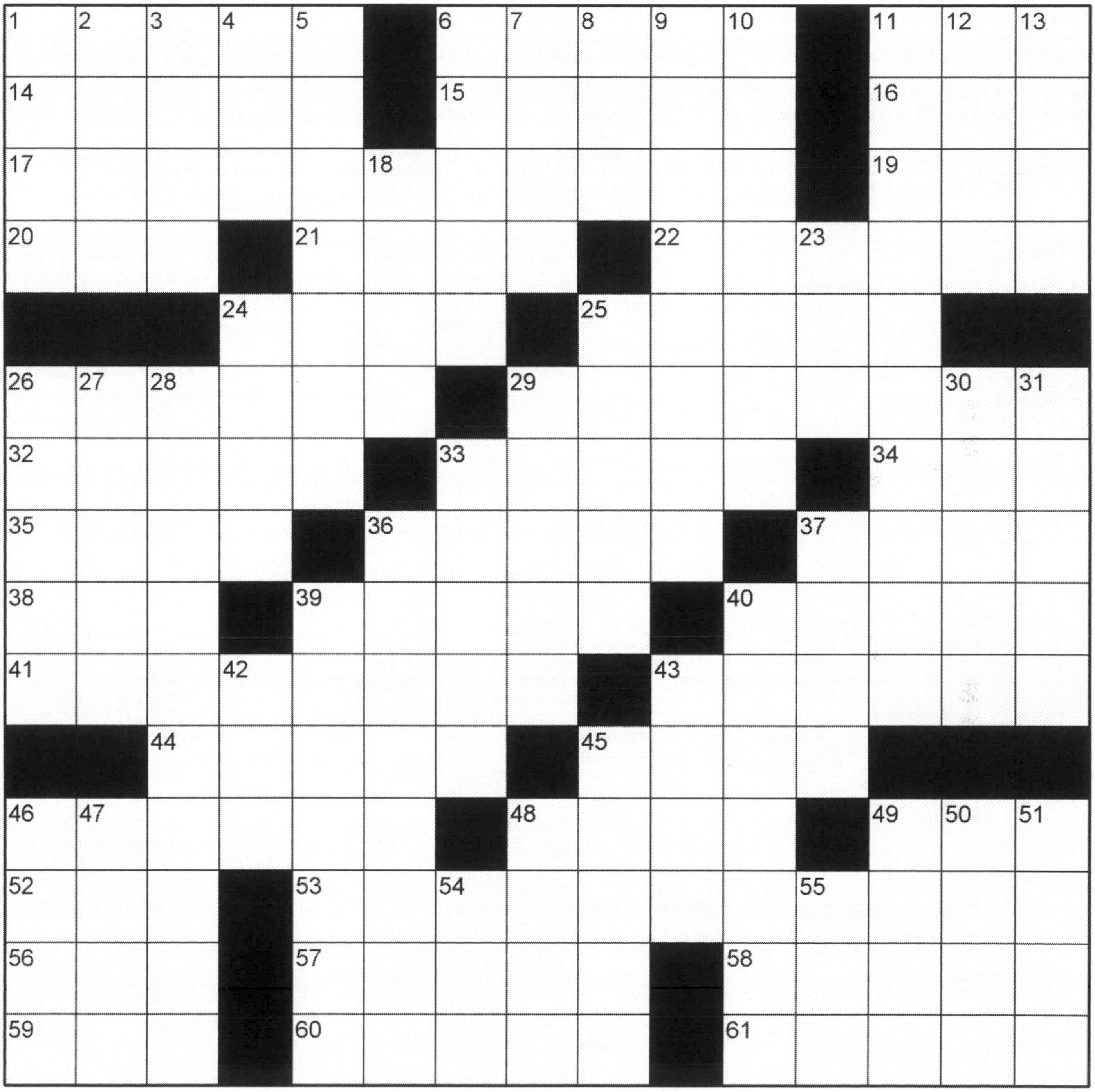

Puzzle 41

ACROSS
1. Provides with food
6. Fragrant oil
11. Govt. agency that has your number
14. Cub leader
15. Rent agreement
16. Bout stopper, for short
17. Heavenly
19. "Ich bin ___ Berliner"
20. 6-pointers
21. Coal-rich German region
22. Recorded
24. Takes a seat
25. Knot
26. Magpie lark
29. Plume
32. Mistake
33. Out of favor
34. Possessed
35. Med school subj.
36. Poker stakes
37. Canon competitor
38. Free
39. Deletion marks in printing
40. Automaton
41. Unhurried
43. Woodland deities
44. "Orphée" painter
45. Bulk
46. German military camp
48. Ore deposit
49. Extrasensory perception
52. To hit a ball high
53. Bright ideas
56. The Braves, on scoreboards
57. Father of Leah and Rachel
58. Available, in a way
59. Honey insect
60. Abrasive substance
61. Fencing needs

DOWN
1. Datum
2. Managed, with "out"
3. Long fish
4. Hand (out)
5. More impertinent
6. Assumed name
7. Rip
8. 1960's chess champ
9. Provided that
10. Name given to the fox
11. Furtively
12. Jump lightly
13. First class (1-3)
18. British National Gallery
23. Certain numero
24. Study
25. Scoffs
26. Oyster gem
27. "Sesame Street" Muppet
28. Able to be exterminated
29. Chipped in
30. Potato (Colloq)
31. Dutch exports
33. Bay
36. Airmail letter
37. Dust speck
39. Hard wearing
40. Newspaper
42. The sun
43. Caesar and others
45. Familiar term for young lad
46. Thick slice
47. Carry
48. Person who lies
49. "House of Frankenstein" director ___ C. Kenton
50. Barrie baddie
51. Attention-getters
54. "How to Succeed in Business Without Really Trying" librettist Burrows
55. "Alley ___!"

Puzzle 42

ACROSS
1. Wild rose
6. Bouquets
11. "Baudolino" author
14. Baseball Hall-of-Famer Combs
15. Supple
16. Resinous deposit
17. Effeminate
19. Newt
20. Simple fastener
21. Eurasian crow
22. Weight measures
24. God: Sp.
25. Annual horse race in England
26. Monastery heads
29. Constituent
32. Slant
33. Group of eight
34. Nigerian native
35. Cloy
36. Soundless
37. Barge
38. Louse egg
39. Exposed
40. Civil War general
41. More prying
43. Coiled
44. Tight-fisted

person
45. Flying mammals
46. Vote
48. Intestinal parts
49. Sharp projection
52. Frozen water
53. Establishment for the old and feeble (7.4)
56. Cries of surprise
57. Icons
58. In-box contents
59. French pronoun
60. Bogotá babies
61. Composition for nine

DOWN
1. Units of loudness
2. Shower
3. "___ la Douce"
4. Peak
5. Redraft a letter
6. Hodgepodges
7. Circular plate
8. His "4" was retired
9. Variable electrical controller, such as a fan or volume control
10. Tempted
11. Concerned with generated power
12. Diner
13. Fall times: Abbr.

18. Little hoppers
23. Egg drink
24. Narcotic
25. Chipped in
26. Grps.
27. Inflammatory swelling
28. Immeasurably deep
29. More gelid
30. Dwelling
31. Mooed
33. External
36. Tranquillity
37. Philly team
39. Constituent of blood serum
40. Radiation, e.g.
42. Petroleum
43. City in NW France
45. Ecstasy
46. Prejudice
47. Continuous dull pain
48. Small island
49. ___ of Arc
50. Friend, to Françoise
51. Cabbage
54. Howard of "Happy Days"
55. Med. care provider

85

ACROSS

1. Performers
6. Belief involving sorcery
11. Little, in Leith
14. Take ___ (travel)
15. ___ cow
16. ___ el Amarna, Egypt
17. Audacious
19. Creek
20. Abilene-to-San Antonio dir.
21. Black bird
22. Academy Awards
24. Paris airport
25. Wet slapping sound
26. Bad luck
29. Estrange
32. Arm joint
33. Place
34. Warning sound
35. Parliament of Poland
36. "From Here to Eternity" wife
37. Restraint
38. You, abroad
39. Earn
40. Grooms hair
41. Congregation
43. Fix in advance
44. Camp shelters
45. Dutch name of The Hague
46. Key of Mozart's "Odense" Symphony
48. Random House cofounder Bennett
49. Fold
52. Cleveland cager, for short
53. Rules
56. Definite article
57. Irish county
58. Bandleader Skinnay ___
59. Sister
60. Trembling poplar
61. Do (Archaic)

DOWN

1. Small amounts
2. Oklahoma tribe
3. ___ Stanley Gardner
4. To free
5. Songbird
6. "Goody!"
7. Tree covering
8. "Die Meistersinger" heroine
9. Moralistic
10. Bothered
11. Schemes
12. Former Israeli P.M.
13. Exclamation to express sorrow
18. Performance by one
23. Is able to
24. Baseball's Blue Moon
25. Rain and snow
26. "Siddhartha" author
27. Kind of acid
28. Goals
29. Heart chambers
30. Clan
31. Artist Max
33. Hindu garments
36. Small falcons
37. "The Witches" director Nicolas
39. One of the Islas Baleares
40. Made
42. Pet form of Leonard
43. Prefix, beyond
45. Trojan beauty
46. Performs
47. When repeated, a fish
48. Remedy
49. Solitary
50. Cuckoos
51. Surreptitious, attention getting sound
54. Breach
55. Rescuer of Odysseus, in myth

Puzzle 44

ACROSS

1. Long distances
6. Excrete
11. Cause of some shaking
14. African musical instrument
15. Flood embankment
16. Want-ad letters
17. Tight-fistedness
19. Mineral spring
20. Colo. is on it
21. Ember
22. Come by
24. Brewing ingredients
25. Ornamental coronet
26. Hyrax
29. Surprising
32. Capable of flowing
33. Thorny
34. Sally Field's "Norma ___"
35. Tibetan monk
36. Worries
37. Hoarfrost
38. 20's dispenser
39. Bundle of cereal plants
40. Skeleton
41. Cutting teeth
43. Pôrto ___, Brazil
44. Bores out
45. Victory: Ger.
46. Flower part
48. Old Fords
49. - Chi. Slow moving martial art form
52. Dockworkers' org.
53. Resembling a tree in size
56. Game with matchsticks
57. Zeus changed her to stone
58. "Women Who Run With the Wolves" author
59. Two-up bat
60. Ladle
61. Painter Andrea del ___

DOWN

1. "Tasty!"
2. Sacred Egyptian bird
3. Catalogue
4. Before
5. Fleshy
6. Sewing machine inventor Howe
7. Robt. E. Lee, e.g.
8. First woman
9. Court sittings
10. State of being testate
11. Feeling hopelessness
12. Pith helmet
13. - Connery
18. Bound
23. Mork's planet
24. Early Chinese dynasty
25. Burglar
26. C sharp
27. Winged
28. Camp for children
29. Mine prop
30. Dubber
31. Large duck-like birds
33. Composer Camille Saint-___
36. Imaginary
37. Film director Nicolas
39. Tribal V.I.P.'s
40. Consecrates
42. Golfers mound
43. Helper
45. ___ throat
46. Skating area
47. Others, to Ovid
48. American grey wolf
49. Four: Prefix
50. Turn ___ profit
51. "Wishing won't make ___"
54. Jeer
55. 11-member grp.

ACROSS
1. Ties
6. Australian marsupial
11. South Africa's ___ Paul Kruger
14. Accustom
15. Force forward
16. "60 Minutes" network
17. Art studies
19. Gear tooth
20. Gold units: Abbr.
21. "Put ___ writing"
22. More slow-witted
24. Cripple
25. Drilled
26. "Dixie" composer
29. Widows
32. One who is paid
33. Singer Rimes
34. Cultural org.
35. Angered
36. "Designing Women" co-star
37. Let it stand
38. "Silent" prez
39. MS. enclosures
40. Rob
41. Difficult problem
43. Having stabiliser fin
44. Metal spikes

45. Musical group
46. Seafood dish
48. Every
49. Literary monogram
52. "Krazy" one
53. Legislatures
56. "The Sultan of Sulu" writer
57. Suffix, diminutives
58. Eleniak of "Baywatch"
59. Spread out for drying
60. Relaxes
61. 1978 Peace Nobelist

DOWN
1. Cheat
2. "Put a lid ___!"
3. Central points
4. "___ Day" (1993 rap hit)
5. Arranged in series
6. Middle East rug
7. Arab League member
8. 30-day mo.
9. Disappointments (3-5)
10. Election loser
11. Western
12. Hautboy
13. Religious title:

Abbr.
18. Arguing
23. Wooden pin
24. Reward
25. Water craft
26. Heroic tales
27. Corday's victim
28. Medullated
29. Dissuade
30. Bailiff
31. Cloyed
33. Is defeated
36. Mitigate
37. Propagative part of a plant
39. Captain
40. Gives a new name
42. Eccentric shaft
43. New Zealand parrot
45. Ecstasy
46. Card game
47. Juniper
48. "Why should ___ you?"
49. "Idylls of the King" character
50. Aleutian island
51. E.T.S. offering
54. A.C.L.U. concerns: Abbr.
55. An age

Puzzle 46

ACROSS
1. Bits
6. Compel
11. Meadow
14. Decorated Murphy
15. "___ Frome"
16. Neither Rep. nor Dem.
17. City in SE Tennessee
19. Fur scarf
20. Bitter vetch
21. "Bill & ___ Excellent Adventure"
22. Contacts quickly, perhaps
24. Some cameras: Abbr.
25. Prayer starter
26. Malay island
29. Shirt fabric
32. Backward
33. Portents
34. And not
35. A carol
36. Young child (Colloq)
37. French silk
38. Finish
39. Charger
40. Scene of W.W. I fighting
41. Tarried
43. Mouthed off
44. Bandaged
45. Sgts. and cpls.
46. Popular record label
48. Grumble
49. Congeal
52. Nigerian native
53. Uncertainty
56. "Oysters ___ season"
57. "Lovergirl" singer ___ Marie
58. Make into an act
59. Cousin of -trix
60. "Frasier" dog
61. Vetches

DOWN
1. Fresh-water fish
2. Essen's river
3. Argonaut who slew Castor
4. Piece
5. Colonist
6. Wards off
7. Platte River people
8. 17th letter of the Greek alphabet
9. Bird that is kept in a cage
10. Captivates
11. Lustful
12. Form of ether
13. Nabokov heroine and others
18. Air (prefix)
23. Talent
24. Catch
25. 1977 George Burns film
26. Swiss city
27. Maine college town
28. Musical interpretations
29. Fathered
30. Sound
31. Avarice
33. Haste
36. Ran
37. Tres y tres
39. Divided by a septum
40. Small satellite
42. Brits' thank-yous
43. March Madness org.
45. Star bursts
46. Suffix with million
47. Baseball stats
48. Prefix for small
49. Growl
50. "___ homo"
51. Allows
54. Cot
55. Disney deer

Puzzle 47

ACROSS
1. Small hand drum
6. Open space in Italian town
11. Stephen of "Michael Collins"
14. Entangled with
15. Sen. Hatch
16. Go wrong
17. Transparent to radiation
19. Simple fastener
20. Suffix with mock
21. Expression used when accident happens
22. A sacramental anointing
24. Corp. money managers
25. Abode of the dead
26. Pacify
29. Regnant
32. Friendship
33. Gambling game
34. Classified ad abbr.
35. Strikes
36. Jargon
37. Biting insect
38. Flawed somehow: Abbr.
39. Military plane acronym
40. Pelvic bones
41. Opinion opener
43. Ideally

44. Apple gizmo
45. Kill
46. Container in which infusions are made
48. Advance money
49. ___ 180
52. Part of a circle
53. They're loaded
56. Law, in Lyon
57. Thomas of the N.B.A.
58. Poets' feet
59. Hallucinogenic drug
60. Natters
61. Crucifix

DOWN
1. Weight allowance
2. Distant
3. Corpse
4. Him, to Henri
5. Reservedly
6. Masterstrokes
7. Parentheses, e.g.
8. G.I. chow in Desert Storm
9. Nipping
10. Busy
11. Power to quickly recover from setback
12. Sea eagles
13. "My Name Is ___" (William Saroyan story collection)

18. Appear threateningly
23. Palillo of "Welcome Back, Kotter"
24. Felines
25. Combs et al.
26. Coastal Brazilian state
27. Eastern V.I.P.'s
28. Occurring in citrus fruit
29. Act in response
30. Approaches
31. Reached
33. British P.M. Tony
36. Somewhat sweet
37. Fool
39. Like some exercises
40. Containing tin
42. Saturate
43. Wings: Lat.
45. Second-year students, for short
46. Lofty
47. Greek god of love
48. Future atty.'s exam
49. Demonstration
50. Eyeballs
51. Garage sale warning
54. Actress Scala
55. ___ es Salaam

Puzzle 48

ACROSS
1. Political pawn González
6. Yoga posture
11. Marvelous, in slang
14. Traditional portion of Muslim law
15. Backs of necks
16. Wood sorrel
17. Easy target
19. 66, e.g.: Abbr.
20. Immigrant's course: Abbr.
21. Be defeated
22. Bird of prey
24. "Norma Rae" director
25. Bee product
26. Remove bones
29. Takes back
32. Hurl
33. French queen, - Antoinette
34. Certain investment, for short
35. Italian currency
36. Cloys
37. ___ the finish
38. N.S. clock setting
39. Japanese wrestlers
40. Crinkled fabric
41. Native of Tahiti
43. Flew high

44. Schemes
45. Egg holders: Abbr.
46. Characteristically French
48. "Moby-Dick" captain
49. Archipelago unit: Abbr.
52. Pier grp.
53. The production of maps
56. Comfy footwear
57. Rights org.
58. Hand out
59. ___ Dee River
60. Precedes
61. Unseals

DOWN
1. To be, to Brutus
2. San ___ Obispo, Calif.
3. Like JFK
4. Social insect
5. Hammering metal spikes in
6. Anguish
7. "Smooth Operator" singer
8. Kwik-E-Mart clerk on "The Simpsons"
9. Mortification
10. Sideways
11. Prospector of 1849
12. Part of a Spanish play

13. 1930's heavyweight champ Max
18. Short letter
23. Architect I. M. ___
24. Author Jaffe
25. "___ Johnny!"
26. Key of Prokofiev's first piano concerto
27. "I Still See ___" ("Paint Your Wagon" tune)
28. Place of origin
29. Betray, in a way
30. Hang
31. Satisfied
33. Mothers
36. Piece of luggage
37. Nest eggs, briefly
39. Impassive
40. With vigor
42. Unwell
43. Male deer
45. 3 Meat cuts
46. Hobbling gait
47. Agave
48. Hardly any
49. ___ dixit
50. Avoid
51. Strong cleaners
54. ___ Victor
55. Viper

96

Puzzle 48

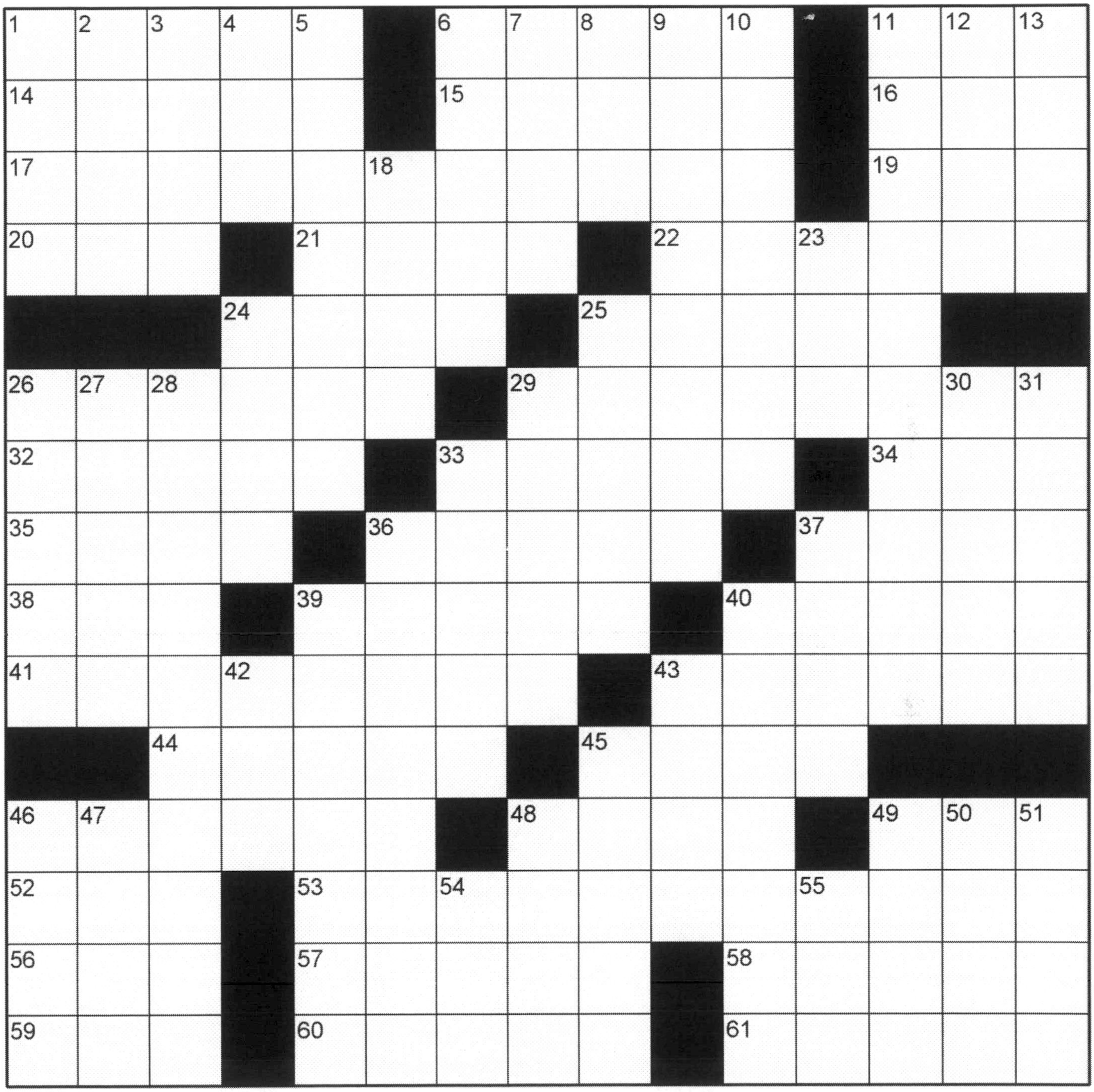
1 2 3 4 5 6 7 8 9 10 11 12 13
14 15 16
17 18 19
20 21 22 23
24 25
26 27 28 29 30 31
32 33 34
35 36 37
38 39 40
41 42 43
44 45
46 47 48 49 50 51
52 53 54 55
56 57 58
59 60 61

Puzzle 49

ACROSS
1. Cavalry sword
6. Scorch
10. Marine mammal
14. "South Pacific" hero
15. Australian super-model
16. "Shave ___ haircut"
17. Cancelation
19. Neighbor of Minn.
20. Sound of a cow
21. Sword-shaped
22. Aspiration
23. Against
24. Titans
26. Place of imprisonment
31. Asserts
32. Appends
33. Indian dish
36. Legumes
37. "A Delicate Balance" playwright
39. Unit of computer memory
40. Illustrative craft
41. Vigor
42. ___ Domingo
43. Woman who owns a business
46. Radiant

49. Bleats
50. Rock's Motley ___
51. Shoelace tips
54. Twice
57. Basketball Hall-of-Famer Harshman
58. Time pieces?
60. Fencing sword
61. Monetary unit of Peru
62. Applause
63. Cong. period
64. ___ Grande, Ariz.
65. Girl's playthings

DOWN
1. Thin stratum
2. Early pulpit
3. Pen
4. "Don't Bring Me Down" grp.
5. Rulers
6. Becomes established
7. "East of Eden" director Kazan
8. All the time
9. Turncoat
10. Walk nonchalantly
11. ___ a high note
12. Change to suit
13. Tarns
18. Poker stake

23. Affectation
25. Apr. addressee
26. Father
27. Always
28. Trim
29. Small drum
30. Carp-like fish
33. Unit of force
34. Firm parts: Abbr.
35. Composer Janácek
37. Fragrant
38. Mouth part
39. Obstructs
41. Brassiere
42. Stowed away
43. Annoys
44. Spain and Portugal
45. Consumes
46. Pinnacles
47. Wine source
48. Baits
52. Actress Rowlands
53. Back muscles, for short
54. Ringing instrument
55. Not rom.
56. Fast fliers
59. "Baudolino" author

Puzzle 50

ACROSS

1. Groom oneself
6. Serene
10. Consider
14. Best
15. Intestinal parts
16. Ancient Peruvian
17. Modernisation (of a house)
19. Beer (Colloq)
20. Supporter of arms, for short
21. Message
22. Valuable metal
23. Singer
24. ___ Island, Fla.
26. Short-lived success
31. Finicky
32. Explorer John and others
33. Soft shoe
36. Half court game?
37. Mildew
39. - Lisa
40. John, Paul and George: Abbr.
41. Dairy property
42. Educate
43. School for young children
46. Simple life form
49. British nobleman
50. East Indies palm
51. Irritates
54. 50's political monogram
57. Grow together
58. Particular places
60. Carson's successor
61. Explorer called "the Red"
62. Kind of chair
63. Paradise
64. Ed.'s request
65. Charlotte ___

DOWN

1. Pornography (Colloq)
2. Sorry sort
3. Sicilian volcano
4. Tokyo, formerly
5. Something new
6. Lemon-like fruit
7. Et ___
8. City NNW of Madrid
9. Decreed
10. WW 1 Australian soldier
11. Register
12. Dangerous strain
13. A Gabor sister
18. Intro drawing class
23. Golfer Isao ___
25. Mothers
26. Healthful retreats
27. Knife handle
28. Wood sorrels
29. Clotted fluid
30. "Do the Right Thing" pizzeria owner
33. Water filled barricade
34. At one time
35. "High Hopes" lyricist
37. Handcuffs
38. W.A. river
39. Blackbird
41. White lie
42. Large-eyed, Indonesian monkey
43. Silent movies star, Buster -
44. Restore facade
45. Erse
46. Leg joint
47. Excavated ore
48. Think
52. Israeli round dance
53. Galatea's love
54. Becomes dark
55. G.P.A. spoilers
56. To be, to Tiberius
59. Greek letter

ACROSS

1. Major artery
6. Tides that attain the least height
10. Openings
14. Guides
15. Lambs: Lat.
16. Land measure
17. Cutting apart for examination
19. Music synthesiser
20. Peak
21. Good things
22. Capital of Moravia
23. Leading player
24. Butchers' offerings
26. Fortunate
31. Renaissance fiddle
32. Scottish Celt
33. Coolers, for short
36. Have ___ (be connected)
37. Disorder
39. The Crimson Tide, familiarly
40. Make lace
41. Malay rice dish, - goreng
42. Parlor game
43. Abstainers from alcohol
46. Farewells
49. Small particle
50. Scene of first miracle
51. Changes to suit
54. Expression of contempt
57. Heavy stick
58. A regenerate state
60. "Gone With the Wind" plantation
61. Like some profs.
62. One -, prejudiced
63. Carol
64. Broadcasts
65. Café cup

DOWN

1. "Betsy's Wedding" star
2. Trompe l'___
3. Grate
4. N.F.L. scores
5. Sterile
6. Character
7. Protection
8. "Green Gables" girl
9. Swine enclosures
10. Frolic
11. Oak nut
12. Prostrate
13. Utah lilies
18. Dressed
23. Cinematographer Nykvist
25. ___ Harbour, Fla.
26. Duff
27. Sofer of soaps
28. Funeral notice
29. Author Marsh
30. Eastern "way"
33. River in central Switzerland
34. U.S.N. rank
35. Sauce
37. Roman capital of Palestine
38. D.D.E.'s predecessor
39. Ointment
41. Modern: Ger.
42. Nearest
43. Infusion sachet
44. Becomes narrow
45. Env. notation
46. Bank holdings: Abbr.
47. ___ Lama
48. Inter ashes
52. Moore of "G.I. Jane"
53. Maturing agent
54. Stench
55. Beats by tennis service
56. London's ___ Park
59. Estuary

Puzzle 52

ACROSS
1. Snub
6. Coarsely ground corn
10. Suffix with poet
14. Jack of "The Great Dictator"
15. Queen who wrote "Leap of Faith"
16. A Chaplin
17. Lack of elegance
19. Raised platform
20. Secular
21. Clergyman
22. Pinnacle
23. Genuine
24. One of two
26. Chance happening
31. Tests
32. Apiece
33. Overact
36. Gym set
37. Humiliate
39. D.C. group
40. Four Monopoly properties: Abbr.
41. Auricular
42. ___ Games
43. Specialist in psychology
46. Accident

49. Egypt's river
50. Gooey (Colloq)
51. Existing
54. Tre + tre
57. Ceases living
58. General assembly?
60. Et ___
61. Last of a Latin trio
62. "The Sopranos" restaurateur
63. Synchronize
64. NASA craft
65. Torment

DOWN
1. Dirt
2. Grandmother
3. ___-doke
4. Petroleum
5. Wigwams
6. Garden pests
7. First-class
8. Soft shoes
9. Sham
10. Salt of iodic acid
11. Train
12. Varnish resin
13. Light beam
18. Grandmother
23. Tach readings
25. "___ bin ein Berliner"

26. German, Mr
27. Woodman
28. Nipples
29. Instruct
30. Small batteries
33. "___ soit qui mal y pense"
34. Anthologies
35. People in charge: Abbr.
37. Abnormal
38. Ballpoint biro
39. Bird prison
41. Mama bear, in Madrid
42. European weasel
43. Laxative
44. Beginnings
45. Catalog
46. King with golden touch
47. Gelidly
48. Loose coil of yarn
52. Title
53. Dutch cheese
54. Mex. miss
55. Certain Prot.
56. "Amazing Grace" ending
59. Metal-bearing mineral

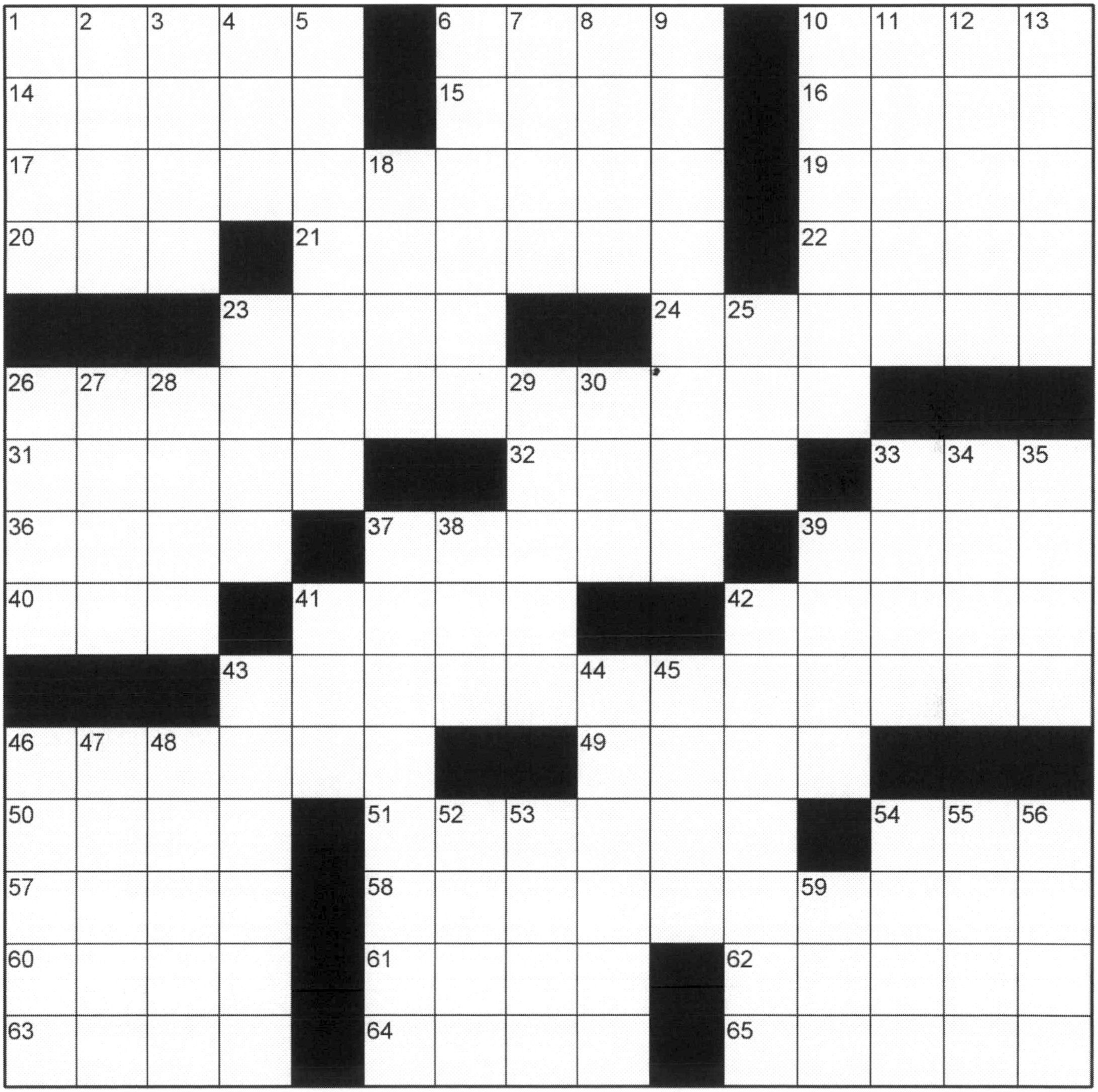

Puzzle 53

ACROSS

1. Refreshment stand
6. Hot Springs and others
10. Arrived
14. Smell
15. Melody
16. Cain's victim
17. Dried berry of the pepper plant
19. Broten of hockey fame
20. Owns
21. Blended
22. Anklebones
23. Parmenides' home
24. Fourth highest peak in the world
26. Arrhythmia
31. Nut of an oak
32. Tarn
33. Can. province
36. Food fish
37. Firearm
39. Strong woody fiber
40. Chemical suffix
41. "Me neither"
42. Throws
43. Art of composing ballets
46. Emphatic form of it
49. Humble
50. Large almost tailless rodent
51. Of a direct ancestor
54. Airline to Stockholm
57. Collections
58. Leaving to live in another country
60. Trigonometric function
61. Mex. title
62. Fortune-telling cards
63. Disrespectful back talk
64. Legis. meeting
65. Equalises

DOWN

1. 19th letter of the Hebrew alphabet
2. Notion
3. Exclamation of mild dismay
4. Dine
5. Russian governmental building
6. Sacred observances
7. Forage
8. Suffix with million or zillion
9. Arenaceous
10. Small territorial district
11. Skip ___
12. Eating occasions
13. "Dallas" matriarch Miss
18. Spool
23. Blunders
25. Gardening tool
26. Visage
27. Image
28. Portend
29. 1966 Michael Caine role
30. 60's chess champ
33. Insect feeler
34. Book after Neh.
35. ___-bitsy
37. Having no roof
38. Like some vbs.
39. Bill
41. Art Ross Trophy org.
42. Clergyman
43. Stops
44. Certain sorority women
45. Cog
46. "No bid"
47. Patty Hearst's name in the S.L.A.
48. Peruses
52. Nagy of Hungary
53. Things to pick
54. Male parent
55. Soon
56. Certain NCO's
59. 23rd letter of the Hebrew alphabet

107

Puzzle 54

ACROSS
1. Clamp
6. Elevator man
10. Vamp Theda
14. Rest atop
15. Actress ___ Flynn Boyle
16. Was indebted
17. Lots and lots
19. Incursion
20. Utter
21. Oval-shaped tablet
22. Sea eagle
23. Agitate
24. Containing tetraethyllead
26. Unmarried woman
31. Pretentious sort
32. Killer whale
33. Eccentric wheel
36. Beauvais's department
37. Become cheerful
39. Table d'___
40. Consume
41. Indian pulses
42. Sealy competitor
43. Reallocation
46. Continental sausage
49. So-so grades
50. Jai ___
51. Narrate verse

54. Italian monk
57. Engage in logrolling
58. Muscular substance of the heart
60. "Bus Stop" playwright
61. Seed cover
62. TV's "Kate & ___"
63. Require
64. Hawaiian goose
65. Adolescent years

DOWN
1. "Gil ___"
2. Baltic capital
3. Ethereal
4. Cedar Rapids college
5. Made law
6. Veteran
7. Old Chinese money
8. Dies ___
9. Block of salt
10. Northern
11. Bestow
12. Marie Antoinette, e.g.
13. Summed
18. Hindmost part of an animal
23. "Leaving Las Vegas" actress

25. Period of history
26. Lodge letters
27. Largest continent
28. Girdle
29. Vexes
30. Watchdog's warning
33. Heart
34. Envelope abbr.
35. Flesh
37. Presiding officer
38. Possesses
39. Garment edges
41. Like L.B.J.
42. Pooh-pooh
43. Fulminated
44. Tapering mass of ice
45. Japanese wooden clog
46. Polio vaccine developer
47. Dress which flares from top (1-4)
48. Immense
52. Australian explorer
53. Money
54. Dossier
55. Wreck
56. Cathy ___, "East of Eden" wife
59. Hand (out)

Puzzle 55

ACROSS
1. Ciphers
6. From a distance
10. F.D.R.'s Scottie
14. Capital of Guam, old-style
15. Annoyed
16. Frozen treats
17. Causing irritation
19. Cloistered women
20. Large body of water
21. Slurred
22. Have ___ for
23. Small remnant
24. Eucharist plates
26. Capital of Madagascar
31. Modern workout system
32. Thick cord
33. Some appliances
36. Budding entrepreneurs, for short
37. The cream
39. Nip
40. J.F.K. arrival
41. Extent of space
42. Sealy rival
43. Unfavorable
46. Spanish royalty
49. Press clothes
50. Current month
51. Axilla
54. "Foucault's Pendulum" author
57. Instance
58. Proprietor of a bookstore
60. Aqueduct of Sylvius, e.g.
61. Actress Singer of "Footloose"
62. Tree exudation
63. Teutonic turndown
64. English public school
65. Musty

DOWN
1. Tins
2. Double curve
3. Information
4. M.D.'s specialty
5. Seaport in SW Italy
6. Allot
7. Nourishment
8. French weapon
9. Organ part
10. All done
11. Sharp
12. Russian revolutionary leader
13. Clubs: Abbr.
18. Zeno of ___
23. Small amounts, as of cream
25. Greeting
26. Modern mall features
27. Bags
28. Nipple
29. Opera solos
30. Decay
33. Copter's forerunner
34. "___, Brute?"
35. Oceans
37. Able to be rubbed out
38. Monetary unit of Romania
39. Hippie gathering of a sort
41. Alicia of "Falcon Crest"
42. Diving ducks
43. Imprison
44. Small earthen pot
45. Eye part
46. Powder from castor-oil plant
47. Related maternally
48. Japanese immigrant
52. Origin
53. 1960's-70's Italian P.M.
54. "Born Free" lioness
55. Line roof
56. Caen's river
59. Allow

Puzzle 55

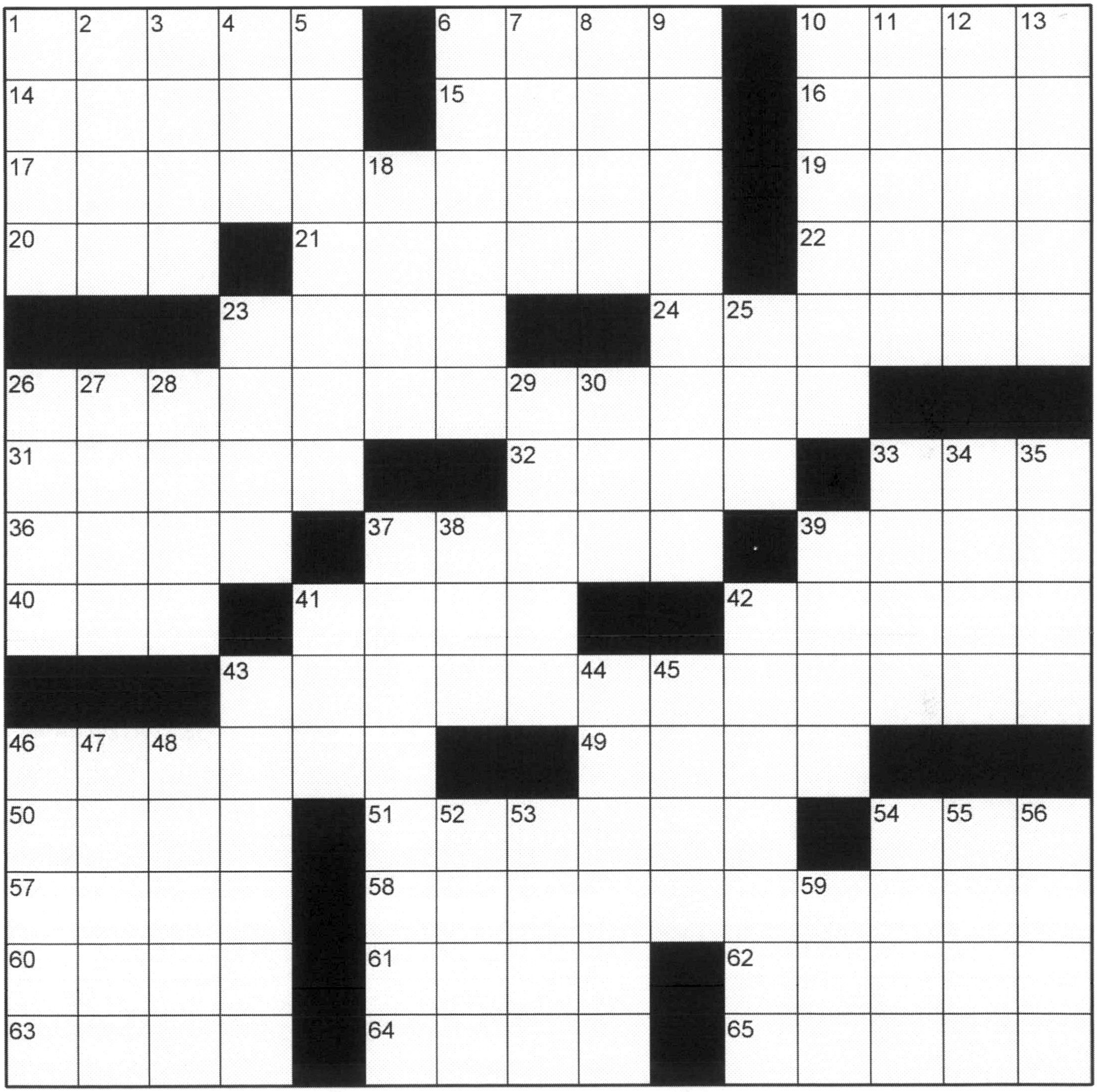

Puzzle 56

ACROSS

1. Borden bovine
6. Peak
10. Identical
14. Bread buns
15. Raccoon
16. Biographer Ludwig
17. Of unknown cause
19. Cartel city
20. Open mesh fabric
21. New World songbird
22. Greek H's
23. Motor car
24. Violet antiseptic
26. See circles
31. Over
32. Pituitary hormone
33. Ballot abbr.
36. Elizabeth of "La Bamba"
37. Menu
39. Italian city
40. Publishers' hirees, for short
41. Neighbor of Libya
42. Distance runner
43. Loose joints
46. Hunting expedition
49. Old Indian coin
50. Lyrical
51. Phoenician of Greek myth
54. Kind of approval
57. Every which way
58. Of horsemanship
60. Female horse
61. Goes to law
62. As a friend, to François
63. May event, for short
64. "Mon Oncle" star
65. Badger-like carnivore

DOWN

1. Ireland
2. Veinlike deposit
3. Narrow aperture
4. 1969 Peace Prize grp.
5. Marry
6. Deed
7. Small salmon
8. Drudge
9. Pregnant
10. Formally withdraw from
11. Cremona artisan
12. Where "Otello" premiered
13. "Fur ___" (Beethoven dedication)
18. Johnson of "Laugh-In"
23. Part of T.A.E.
25. Scottish expression
26. Practical joke
27. In bed
28. Charged particles
29. Afternoon: Sp.
30. Outside: Prefix
33. Rhythmic swing
34. "Got it"
35. Poet
37. Best of the best
38. Some batteries
39. ___ colada
41. Minced oath
42. Cathedral
43. Servile follower
44. Son of Mary Stuart
45. Responsibility
46. "Me, too!"
47. Pitcher, of a sort
48. Norwegian estuary
52. Blue shade
53. Performance by two
54. Decree
55. Knight's wife
56. Indigo
59. Cellular stuff

Puzzle 57

ACROSS
1. Crocodiles (Colloq)
6. Avis adjective
10. Bag
14. Nectar
15. Carolina college
16. Designer von Furstenberg
17. Malignant (4-6)
19. Wallaroo
20. Greeted
21. Gratify
22. Depression in a surface
23. Olio
24. A monkey
26. Removed from ownership
31. English Derby city
32. Separate article
33. Literary inits.
36. 1990's Senate majority leader
37. Former German state
39. River in central Switzerland
40. Commercials
41. Stable attendant
42. Borders
43. Remove as too old
46. Swiss city
49. English monk
50. Tel ___, Israel
51. Adventurous expedition

54. Colorful form of the common carp
57. Narrow country road
58. Spices
60. ___ 'acte (intermission)
61. "Das Lied von der ___"
62. Bright glow
63. "But, ___ was ambitious, I slew him": Brutus
64. Performer
65. Ranee's wrap

DOWN
1. H.S. class
2. Wander
3. "Step ___!"
4. Animation unit
5. Indicator of illness
6. Modernises
7. "Crimes and Misdemeanors" actor
8. Some deer
9. Hans Christian
10. Sowed
11. Fits
12. Horn-shaped bone
13. Ravels
18. Martinique et Guadeloupe
23. Dot
25. Garment edge

26. Crème ___ crème
27. Modern music holder
28. High fliers
29. Downy duck
30. Bernadette, e.g.: Abbr.
33. Insane
34. Cy Young winner Saberhagen
35. Zaire's Mobutu ___ Seko
37. Detoured around
38. Top card
39. Together, on a score
41. Blazer, e.g.
42. Finishes
43. Harsh
44. Bully, often
45. Emperor of Rome 54-68
46. Hood-shaped anatomical part
47. Editor Harold
48. Coming between 8 and 10
52. Prefix, air
53. Lose colour
54. Knot in wood
55. Barbarous person
56. "Gotcha"
59. Dockworker's org.

Puzzle 58

ACROSS
1. Mil. addresses
5. Cannabis
10. Moist
14. Heroine of Tennessee Williams's "Summer and Smoke"
15. Pastoral
16. Having wings
17. Top dog
19. Gershwin's "The ___ Love"
20. Capital of Chile
21. Lassoing
23. Rum
24. Flute
25. Bottom
27. Detachment
32. Some beans
33. Alone
34. Exclamation of surprise
35. Askew
36. Actor, - Karloff
37. Russian secret police
38. Never, in Nuremberg
39. An Indian
40. Strand, in a way
41. Tyranny
43. Reddish brown chalcedony
44. "___ girl!"
45. The (German)

46. Purpose
49. See circled squares
54. High-pitched tone
55. Letters of commendation
57. Capable
58. Mother-in-law of Ruth
59. Rat tail?
60. Black, as la nuit
61. Lazy -, revolving serving tray
62. Musical notes

DOWN
1. Exclamations of surprise
2. Prayer
3. Arabian Peninsula country
4. "Unfortunately ..."
5. Wide
6. Suspended
7. "Giovanna d'___" (Verdi opera)
8. "Bad idea"
9. Admirable
10. Make moist
11. Kyrgyzstan range
12. "Buddenbrooks" author
13. Prude
18. Conceals
22. Ices

24. Lamella
25. ___ State (Arkansas nickname)
26. Actor Lew
27. Tone deafness
28. Noblemen
29. Enthusiastic
30. Savoury
31. Keep away from
32. Beach feature
36. Kinds of heron
37. Egg-shaped musical instruments
39. Have the ___ for
40. Alpine river
42. Very poor person
45. "Beyond the Sea" singer, 1960
46. Israel's Abba
47. Biblical peak
48. Delicatessen
49. Corp. money managers
50. Blood: Prefix
51. Prefix, eight
52. Small dabbling duck
53. J.F.K. arrivals
56. French, water

Puzzle 59

ACROSS
1. 8th letter of the Hebrew alphabet
5. Wiser
10. Barrie buccaneer
14. Requiem Mass word
15. Spry
16. Basics
17. Relish
19. Diplomacy
20. Part of Great Britain
21. Sickness of stomach
23. Sum
24. Religious title: Abbr.
25. Uncommon
27. Pertaining to elements
32. Water-repellent cloth
33. Italian monies
34. ___ Simbel, Egypt
35. Rent-a-car company
36. Virile males
37. Bakery employee
38. Boardroom bigwig
39. Adores
40. Slender part of the leg
41. Student's worry
43. Inner Hebrides island
44. Architect William Van ___
45. Cartoonist Keane
46. Call off
49. Unfit to be eaten
54. Wife of Jacob
55. Inherent
57. "Artaxerxes" composer
58. Related on one's mother's side
59. Swallow
60. Luna
61. Readjust
62. Daze

DOWN
1. Rose fruit
2. ___ the Red
3. Savoury Mexican dish
4. Metric land measures
5. Cold meal
6. Against
7. Coat with gold
8. Former measure of length
9. Harness driver
10. Sixth planet
11. New corp. hires
12. Behold, in old Rome
13. "Cómo ___?"
18. Mayflower Compact signer
22. Matures
24. Smallest
25. Wanders
26. Farewell
27. Cricket team
28. Citrus fruits
29. Sticky
30. White poplar tree
31. Tempt
32. Ornamental fabric
36. Pub manager
37. Suspicions
39. Singer Lovett
40. Stage whisper
42. German cathedral city
45. Procreate
46. Large mollusc
47. Air (prefix)
48. Prefix with second
49. Writer Tarbell and others
50. Evening, in ads
51. Boxing contest
52. Corker
53. "Baseball Tonight" channel
56. Direction opposite SSW

ACROSS

1. Actress Rowlands
5. Implied
10. Hick
14. Incursion
15. Seat of Marion County, Fla.
16. Without ___ (dangerously)
17. Resembling an orchestra
19. Japanese soup
20. Submerged up to the knees
21. Warning horn
23. "Norma ___"
24. In bed
25. Those
27. In dispute
32. Presses clothes
33. Precise
34. French, water
35. Ecstatic
36. Ruse
37. Winter comment
38. "Fables in Slang" author
39. W.W. I soldier
40. Best
41. Tranquillisers
43. Cries of aversion
44. Wool package
45. Greek letter
46. Straight downhill ski run
49. Ancestor
54. Some beans
55. Deli offerings
57. Story
58. Intervening
59. Antarctica's Prince ___ Coast
60. Leading player
61. Form of Spanish "to be"
62. Ooze

DOWN

1. Understand
2. Acquire through merit
3. Pleasing
4. Person who supports a cause
5. Plain ___
6. Entr'___
7. Freshwater fish
8. Dockworker's org.
9. Radio program in wich listeners participate
10. Open shelter
11. Alternative to Windows
12. "Eso ___" (Paul Anka hit)
13. English college
18. Dutch exports
22. Baryshnikov, by birth
24. Counting frame
25. Commerce
26. Wished for
27. Stem from
28. Banish
29. Sleeping car accommodation
30. Fats
31. Wallaroo
32. Nest eggs, briefly
36. Laborious
37. Bugbears
39. Elhi orgs.
40. Exterior
42. Person who ill-treats
45. Sea eagles
46. Concordes
47. Outer garment
48. Tree frog
49. A clenched hand
50. A Chaplin
51. Australian super-model
52. Wings
53. Invitation letters
56. Old video game inits.

Puzzle 61

ACROSS

1. Let fall
5. Bangladesh's capital, old-style
10. Narrow inlets
14. Subtle emanation
15. Bay
16. Old Icelandic literary work
17. Bubonic plague
19. Property title
20. Dotage
21. Jewish fraternity
23. Fish part
24. Snick and ___
25. Hitler's autobiography, "- Kampf"
27. It opened in 1825
32. Inward feeling
33. The whole range
34. Self-esteem
35. Smallest component
36. Fairy tale brother
37. Work units
38. Girl or woman
39. 1980's attorney general
40. A parent
41. Variety of calcite
43. "Big Mouth" Martha
44. Quantities: Abbr.
45. Electrical unit
46. Four-wheeled carriage
49. Strong heavy cotton fabric
54. Musical instrument
55. Return to native land
57. Quiet town
58. Muse of poetry
59. Financial page inits.
60. Male deer
61. Kills
62. Benevolent

DOWN

1. Applies lightly
2. Dominion
3. "The Plague" city
4. Opposition to war
5. Dispatched
6. Without ___ (dangerously)
7. Pottery material
8. Prefix, whale
9. Reading room
10. View from Jidda
11. ___ fixe
12. Capital of Yemen
13. "The Sweetest Taboo" singer
18. "In & Out" star, 1997
22. Cult
24. Boil slowly
25. Dense element
26. Gay leader?
27. Wading birds
28. Lift
29. Square
30. Longhorn rival
31. Bome to be without
32. Heroic story
36. Gesticulates
37. Passing
39. Mother
40. Abalone
42. Good-for-nothing
45. Singers
46. Throws softly
47. Adjoin
48. "A Doll's House" wife
49. Film rating org.
50. Like Cheerios
51. Send to the canvas
52. "Wishing won't make ___"
53. Requirement
56. Schubert's "The ___-King"

Puzzle 62

ACROSS

1. Short pans
5. Spills the beans
10. Lengthy
14. Suffragist Carrie Chapman ___
15. Take in again
16. At sea
17. Completely
19. "Moby Dick" captain
20. Los Angeles suburb
21. An uncertainty
23. Brits' thank-yous
24. Act silently
25. Little, e.g.
27. Isotope of hydrogen
32. Gather
33. Belgian painter James
34. 22.5 degrees
35. Prehistoric sepulchral tomb
36. Lowest point
37. "Bill & ___ Excellent Adventure"
38. ___ Hsi (empress dowager of China during the Boxer Rebellion)
39. Beauty parlour
40. Doughnut-shaped

41. Detaching
43. Table d'___
44. Republic in SW Asia
45. Remove intestines from fish
46. Overcome
49. Central part of a ship
54. Garden pest
55. Excites
57. Beauvais's department
58. Drug obtained from poppies
59. Redact
60. Sauce
61. Author Marsh
62. Fast fleet

DOWN

1. West Coast sch.
2. Festival
3. Start of many addresses
4. Sturdiest
5. Machine-guns
6. Baltic native
7. "But, ___ was ambitious, I slew him": Brutus
8. Hive insect
9. An attendant
10. Encampment
11. Dept. of Labor division
12. Close to
13. Fool
18. Cogs
22. Certain league: Abbr.
24. Pondering
25. Wrong
26. Stroll
27. Buy and sell
28. ___ a high note
29. Lifeless
30. Unwarranted
31. Untidy state
32. Broadway opening
36. Swimming
37. Feet (Colloq)
39. "___ Smile" (1976 hit)
40. Dull sounds
42. Lords
45. Gadget
46. Brit. decorations
47. "East of Eden" director Kazan
48. Bother
49. Capital of Western Samoa
50. Island in central Hawaii
51. Brick carriers
52. Arctic native
53. Attention-getters
56. Automobile sticker fig.

ACROSS
1. Nobleman
5. Platter player
10. On ___ (equipotent)
14. Falco of "The Sopranos"
15. Trojan beauty
16. Travelled on
17. Toilets
19. Dinner or tea
20. Hilton rival
21. Cold and damp
23. Cpl., e.g.
24. Reared
25. Quick glance
27. Suitable
32. Fort ___, Fla.
33. Buy-one-get-one-free item?
34. Tree of the genus Quercus
35. "___ Well That Ends Well"
36. Rimes of country music
37. Twining stem
38. College in Cedar Rapids
39. Sprite
40. Suns
41. Puts at risk
43. Heed
44. Actress Arthur and others
45. Bashful

46. Rare metallic element
49. Slats collectively
54. Couple
55. Brain
57. Australian super-model
58. "Cool!"
59. Movie princess
60. Toboggan
61. Append
62. Go-___

DOWN
1. Long fish
2. Wife of Esau
3. Split
4. Pupils
5. Photograph
6. Champion
7. Lena of "Chocolat"
8. Born
9. In the movies
10. Battle fleet
11. Verse
12. First man
13. Depend
18. Small nails
22. Sly look
24. Salt solutions
25. Support tower
26. Caught congers
27. High points
28. Egg white
29. The capital of Idaho

30. Tall and thin
31. Supplements
32. Club-like weapon
36. Tendon like tissue
37. The words of an infant
39. French tire
40. Voting stall
42. Bore
45. Castrated cockerel
46. Roman dates
47. Void
48. Broad valley
49. Heroin
50. Mother of Apollo
51. Intestinal parts
52. Film ___
53. Midge
56. Grant source: Abbr.

Puzzle 64

ACROSS

1. Part of N.A.A.C.P.: Abbr.
5. Dangerous strain
10. Bickerer in the "Iliad"
14. Kind of platter
15. Fictional salesman
16. Elevator pioneer
17. Rule of the wealthy
19. "Star Wars" name
20. Selenographer
21. South Pacific Island - Capital Papeete
23. Small amount
24. Jerk
25. Wool fibre
27. Cloying
32. "Roxana" author
33. Hammer parts
34. Take to court
35. Alaska's first governor
36. Set up again
37. Lagerlöf's "The Wonderful Adventures of ___"
38. Small cask
39. Greet and seat
40. Distributed cards
41. Evenings
43. ___ and aahs
44. Almost forever
45. 1980's White House nickname
46. Cunning
49. Abnormal egotism
54. Extol
55. Charging with a responsibility
57. Got down from mount
58. Bandleader Skinnay ___
59. One of the Aleutians
60. He sang "I've Got You Under My Skin" with Frank Sinatra on "Duets"
61. Aptly named English novelist
62. Girl

DOWN

1. Stove or washer: Abbr.
2. "Star Trek" navigator
3. Reeled
4. Act of nodding one's head
5. Charlton Heston title role
6. Aboriginal rite
7. Arabian Peninsula land
8. Resinous deposit
9. Any unnamed object
10. Capital of Inner Mongolia
11. Sewing case
12. "Norma Rae" director
13. Italian wine province
18. Papal vestment
22. Latin 101 verb
24. Beer mugs
25. Desert region in S Israel
26. Adult
27. Goes fast
28. Eagle's nest
29. Thomas of the N.B.A.
30. Negates
31. Metrical romance
32. Apollo astronaut Slayton
36. Antlered animals
37. Newborn
39. Pack away
40. Ill-fates
42. Must
45. Stir
46. Thick slice
47. Nimbus
48. Undoing
49. Sicilian volcano
50. Network
51. Naldi of old films
52. Writing fluids
53. "What ___!"
56. GPS heading

Puzzle 65

ACROSS
1. Not genuine: Abbr.
5. Mosque officials
10. Retired fliers
14. Prolonged unconsciousness
15. Chip dip
16. Natter
17. Making lean by wasting away of flesh
19. Part of verb to ride
20. Cover with a veneer
21. City in SW Iran
23. Center X or O
24. Barge
25. Brother of Fidel
27. Formal ball
32. Peasant
33. Winged
34. Big D.C. lobby
35. Trumpet
36. Uneven surface
37. Pace
38. Boise's county
39. Swiss city on the Rhine
40. Surrounding glows
41. Track event
43. Snake, for one
44. Sense
45. Land measure
46. Diocese
49. Commit to memory

54. Chick follower
55. Got rid of
57. Robt. E. Lee, e.g.
58. Sickened
59. Oscar ___ Renta
60. Cornerstone abbr.
61. Fortune 500 company based in Moline, Ill.
62. Small drink of liquor

DOWN
1. NATO member: Abbr.
2. N.Y.C. cultural center
3. Officiating priest of a mosque
4. Not inclined to conversation
5. Son of Abraham
6. Lustreless
7. Sam Shepard's "___ of the Mind"
8. AOL rival
9. Acumen
10. Illegible handwriting
11. Fitted with shoes
12. "Behold!"
13. Submachine gun
18. Collectively
22. Trunk of a tree

24. U-shaped fastener
25. ___ Island Red
26. Pertaining to the ear
27. Pertaining to a cause
28. Ancient Mexican
29. Foreword, for short
30. Mountain nymph
31. Back of neck
32. Scorch
36. Uncovered head
37. Add besides
39. Parting words
40. Brother of Moses
42. Abroad
45. Ammonia derivative
46. Leaf of a book
47. Fruity coolers
48. Hire
49. Long distance
50. Part of E.M.T.: Abbr.
51. Anatomical canal
52. Ward of "Sisters"
53. Yellow cheese coated with red wax
56. Falsehood

131

Puzzle 66

ACROSS
1. Honey liquor
5. Trade agreements
10. Wood sorrels
14. To
15. Grain fungus
16. Part played
17. Friendly
19. "___ Lap" (1983 film)
20. "No kidding!"
21. Pakistani city
23. Switch positions
24. Mountain lion
25. Potato (Colloq)
27. Rectory
32. "Don't make ___!"
33. Fencing equipment
34. Afrique du ___
35. Lake
36. Drays
37. Creole vegetable
38. Moose
39. Legal
40. Music hall
41. Fashionably
43. Bovines
44. Friend
45. Scottish cap
46. Capital of the Bahamas
49. Brunch order
54. Adjoin
55. Putting forward a person's name for election
57. Wan
58. Alter
59. Sewing case
60. Breeding horse
61. Tiers
62. Decomposes

DOWN
1. Certain bond, informally
2. Chemical endings
3. Battling
4. Kennel
5. Things owing
6. Greek god of love
7. Farm prefix
8. Chat room abbr.
9. Needles
10. Parentless child
11. Small salmon
12. Having wings
13. Withered
18. Arm extremities
22. Andy's radio partner
24. Attractive
25. Refine my melting
26. Jaunty
27. Wonderful
28. Fourth month
29. Awry
30. Hindu teachers
31. Dutch cheese
32. Cathy ___, "East of Eden" wife
36. Between earth and moon
37. Distance measuring instrument
39. Wallace of Reader's Digest
40. Central Florida city
42. Endured
45. Nurses
46. Sleeps briefly
47. Blind as ___
48. "Star Trek" helmsman
49. Portent
50. Type of fur
51. Josip Broz, familiarly
52. Carpenter's fastener
53. Auspices
56. Medical suffix

Puzzle 67

ACROSS
1. Jump
5. Soother
10. "If He Walked Into My Life" musical
14. "Beetle Bailey" pooch
15. Frighten
16. 0 on a phone: Abbr.
17. Trying
19. Auditors
20. False teeth
21. Breathe in
23. Pitcher Fernandez
24. The Sun, for example
25. Wood joint
29. Third son of Adam
30. Sick
33. Paddled
34. Burn slightly
35. Short take-off and landing aircraft
36. Drug-yielding plant
37. Strongly fragrant sage
38. Catalan painter Joan
39. Egg holders: Abbr.
40. Large trees
41. Indiana's state flower
42. Torrid
43. Abode
44. Frenzied woman
45. Verbal exams
47. ___ Gardens
48. Enter cautiously
50. Three before seven
55. Wings: Lat.
56. Made sour
58. Breeding horse
59. Booth
60. Money
61. Hearing organs
62. Woefully
63. "___ Coming" (1969 hit)

DOWN
1. Burden
2. Suffix, diminutive
3. Letter abbr.
4. Bard
5. Wit
6. Played the part of
7. "Je ne ___ quoi"
8. Sea eagle
9. Office where specific details are kept
10. Coffee
11. Specter
12. Repast
13. Gaelic
18. Pondered
22. Advanced degree?
24. Cogs
25. Cockroach (Colloq)
26. Finnish architect Alvar ___
27. Huge sauropod dinosaur
28. Hive insects
29. Tremble
31. "___ Doone" (1869 novel)
32. Bridges in movies
34. Large molluscs
35. Bob Hoskins role of 1991
37. Calmness
41. Manhandle
43. "Bali ___"
44. Fittingly
46. Marsh plants
47. Small crustaceans eaten by whales
48. Relax
49. ___ Vista
50. In ___ way
51. Gospel singer Winans
52. Spoken
53. He loved Lucy
54. Old English letters
57. N.Y.C. subway inits.

134

Puzzle 68

ACROSS

1. They're all in the family
5. Harsh Athenian lawgiver
10. Certain herring
14. Paradise
15. Conger catcher
16. Black, as la nuit
17. Assertion made without proof
19. "Das Rheingold" goddess
20. French mathematician
21. Eastern hospice
23. Antipoverty agcy.
24. Ante
25. Grave
29. Small salmon
30. Not
33. Conscious
34. Songs for one
35. Dutch cheese
36. Singer, - Crosby
37. Caper
38. "Unforgettable" singer
39. Finishes
40. Peruse
41. Course
42. Some linemen: Abbr.
43. Egyptian solar deity
44. Government morals protector
45. Person who explores caves
47. Leg
48. Eats grass
50. Mounted soldier
55. Engrossed
56. Favorable
58. "Amazing Grace" ending
59. English race course
60. Monetary unit of Cambodia
61. Gender abbr.
62. Infant's loincloth
63. June 6, 1944

DOWN

1. Marine mammal
2. Doing nothing
3. Lux. neighbor
4. Dagger
5. Make numb
6. Back in
7. Sam Shepard's "___ of the Mind"
8. Boardroom bigwig
9. Pertaining to birds
10. Slink
11. Dreadful
12. Assistant
13. Minor oath
18. Goblin
22. ___ jacket
24. Firm
25. Cavalry sword
26. Unpaid
27. Scenic paintings
28. Energy units
29. Trig function
31. Finnish architect Alvar ___
32. Mideast V.I.P.
34. Deride
35. Nobel Prize subj.
37. Pressurised underground water basin
41. Staff again
43. Greeting
44. Hollow
46. Indian of Mexico
47. Lively dance
48. Harsh
49. Tabula ___
50. Soyuz rocket letters
51. Fat
52. Footnote note
53. Zeno's home
54. Depend
57. Decryption org.

ACROSS

1. Medieval chest
5. Songwriters' org.
10. Part of U.S.N.A.: Abbr.
14. Restrain
15. Capital of Tibet
16. Rescue
17. Moderate form of liberalism
19. Seed covering
20. Exceptional
21. Native Arizonan
23. Like Beethoven's "Pastoral" Symphony
24. Assert
25. Big citrus fruit
29. Matching outfit
30. 1997 U.S. Open winner
33. Grey
34. Strange person
35. Scheme
36. Islamic call to prayer
37. War hero Murphy
38. Actress Virna
39. Meeting: Abbr.
40. - Connery
41. "Carmen" composer
42. Superlative suffix
43. Part of Nasdaq: Abbr.
44. Absconders
45. Capital of Morocco
47. Hawaii's Mauna ___
48. Ammonia derivatives
50. Rockets
55. Salt
56. Very small amount of money
58. Eastern pooh-bah
59. Icon
60. Send out
61. Son of Ramses I
62. Roman dates
63. Fathers

DOWN

1. Skin eruption
2. Regrets
3. Harvest
4. Showing unusual talent
5. Unnaturally white person
6. Bundle of cereal plants
7. Sagan of "Cosmos"
8. ___ rule
9. Palmy
10. Japanese beer brand
11. Convert into caramel
12. Tel ___
13. Delete (Printing)
18. Coldly
22. Cereal grass
24. Bring up to speed
25. Facet
26. Seeps
27. City in the SE Netherlands
28. Sea eagles
29. Portable chair
31. Intense light beam
32. Fits of rage
34. Visitor
35. Ballet bend
37. Killer
41. An explosion
43. Marge's father-in-law on "The Simpsons"
44. Moats
46. Dwight's opponent in '52 and '56
47. Lord
48. Literary collections
49. Magician
50. Groan
51. Angered
52. Peruvian capital
53. "Idylls of the King" lady
54. Some N.C.O.'s
57. Medical care grp.

ACROSS

1. Labels
5. Rap
10. "___ Baby" ("Hair" song)
14. Well ventilated
15. Composer Boulanger
16. Something that is lost
17. Gradual increases in sound
19. Young male horse
20. Pagans
21. Uncinate
23. Cathedral city
24. Sully
25. Superior of a convent
29. Tim of "WKRP in Cincinnati"
30. Extrasensory perception
33. Spins
34. Equipment
35. Egg-shaped
36. Mars: Prefix
37. Desert plants
38. Hawaiian port
39. Capital of Switzerland
40. Latin 101 word
41. Work dough
42. Droop
43. Crack
44. What
ochlophobes fear
45. Sharp
47. Scooby-___ (cartoon dog)
48. Brewing grain
50. Vermilion
55. Public swimming pool
56. Disorder of the pituitary gland
58. Paradise
59. Sweatbox
60. Chick's tail?
61. Curse
62. "Merry Company" artist
63. To a smaller extent

DOWN

1. Dash gauge
2. Yorkshire river
3. La ___ tar pits
4. Network: Abbr.
5. Genuflects
6. Nurse for children
7. Chances
8. Half of a 1955 merger
9. Inhabitant of Kashmir
10. Big name in kitchen foil
11. Critical analysis of a book
12. Small island
13. Founded: Abbr.
18. Board game
22. Brit. lexicon
24. Chairs
25. Semites
26. Kentucky college
27. Outdoor tavern
28. North Carolina college
29. Sum up
31. Dish of raw vegetables
32. Walks wearily
34. Dry red wine
35. "___ you don't!"
37. Sissy
41. Basic monetary unit of Denmark
43. German pronoun
44. Swindler
46. Exact replica
47. One of the Titans
48. A bubble
49. Turturro of "The Sopranos"
50. Rock's Motley
51. "I've Got ___ in Kalamazoo"
52. Past tense of bid
53. Brews
54. Bar selections
57. Feline

Puzzle 71

ACROSS
1. Sun ray
5. Lariat
10. Modern Maturity org.
14. Capital of Western Samoa
15. Hautboys
16. American Indian
17. Discount again
19. Writer Sarah ___ Jewett
20. Haul under the bottom of a ship
21. "Relativity" artist
23. High-pitched
24. Dangerous
25. Pretense
29. Dietary, in ads
30. Label
33. Egg-shaped
34. Spanish words of agreement (2.2)
35. Clarified butter
36. Verne's submariner
37. Country bumpkins
38. Love, in Lima
39. Let fall
40. Sale caveat
41. Ruse
42. Sun Devils' sch.
43. Future doc's exam
44. Folding top of a carriage
45. Feeble
47. Geometric fig.
48. Regal residence
50. Work clothes
55. Part of USNA
56. Good-for-nothing
58. Aquatic plant
59. Dig
60. Hydroxyl compound
61. Sorry soul
62. Change
63. Donkey's years

DOWN
1. Dog cry
2. Fencing sword
3. Assistant
4. Chain armour
5. Locality
6. Around
7. Inner spirit
8. Monetary unit of Japan
9. Inflammation of bone
10. In a cocked position
11. Irregular heartbeat
12. Mel's "Ransom" costar
13. Equal
18. Ghost
22. Atlanta-to-Miami dir.
24. Dangers
25. "The Grapes of Wrath" star, 1940
26. Asserts
27. Conceal
28. On the top
29. Legal
31. Ages
32. Sleeping car accommodation
34. Agave fibre
35. Erse
37. Large landed estate
41. North Dakota's largest city
43. Family name prefix
44. Coal
46. Navigational aid
47. Bend
48. Allen's successor
49. Censorship-fighting org.
50. Target of a military press
51. Bide-___
52. City in W Nevada
53. North Carolina school
54. Old cloth measures
57. Conger

Puzzle 72

ACROSS
1. Blockheads
5. Prudes
10. Badlands Natl. Park locale
14. Farm prefix
15. Theatrical parody
16. When doubled, a Pacific capital
17. Replant with trees
19. The King's middle name
20. Dismissed
21. No-goodnik
23. Level of karate proficiency
24. Turned towards
25. Ladle
29. Cut ruthlessly
30. Tokyo, once
33. Made a mistake
34. Torture device
35. Shakespeare's river
36. Supplemented, with "out"
37. Day of "Pillow Talk"
38. Actress Taylor
39. Hi-fi spinners: Abbr.
40. Bones
41. Battery brand
42. Writer LeShan
43. Silence
44. Abate
45. Jewish teacher
47. Brown-capped boletus mushroom
48. Faucet
50. Unmarried person
55. Pond
56. Altitudes
58. A hint
59. Busted
60. Sale sign
61. Aide: Abbr.
62. Refine metal
63. Burden

DOWN
1. Paddles
2. "A Death in the Family" writer
3. Kukla, ___ and Ollie
4. Gentle
5. Hawkish
6. Showed film again
7. Actress Judith
8. Astronaut Grissom
9. Blows
10. Digging tool
11. Recklessly brave people
12. Eager
13. Big ape
18. Lost colour
22. "Egad!"
24. Instrument panel
25. Caterpillar competitor
26. Angry
27. Uncertain
28. Walkers, for short
29. Stern
31. Soft
32. Bulb vegetable
34. Big name in wine
35. Guinness and others
37. Skeptics
41. Warehouse
43. "Deadwood" airer
44. East Mediterrranean region
46. Aiguillette
47. Polite
48. Humane org.
49. Successful runners, for short
50. Sand dune
51. Monetary unit of Iran
52. ___ Nostra
53. "National Velvet" author Bagnold
54. Actual being
57. Thrash

ACROSS

1. Dutch name of The Hague
5. "Me, too"
10. Cotton seed vessel
14. Munich's river
15. First name in 2000 news
16. Continent
17. Named
19. Rat-___
20. Words of encouragement
21. Foreign dignitaries
23. Computer giant
24. Brazilian novelist Jorge
25. Bird of prey
29. Dull
30. "Monty Python" airer
33. Laughing dog
34. Shower
35. Blackthorn fruit
36. Res ___ loquitur
37. Fathered
38. Dear, as a signorina
39. Refusals
40. Galatea's love
41. Bottoms
42. F.I.C.A. funds it
43. Movie-rating org.
44. Core
45. Gum
47. Part of verb to be
48. Coop up
50. Salty
55. Cheers
56. "No way!"
58. "Why should ___ you?"
59. Throw
60. Neighbor of Tenn.
61. Bounders
62. S-bends
63. Actress Thompson

DOWN

1. Rube
2. "Hard Road to Glory" author
3. River in central Switzerland
4. Clasp
5. Divan
6. Kind of acid
7. Isn't
8. Actress, - West
9. Popular
10. Bleated
11. Bone-forming cell
12. Fibber
13. Back muscles, for short
18. It won't keep you up
22. Fairy queen
24. Zodiac sign
25. Lower legs
26. Some needles
27. Made a systematic enquiry into a subject
28. Much may follow it
29. "Beavis and Butt-Head" spinoff
31. Wood-eating insect
32. Stop
34. Puerto ___
35. Scrutinize
37. Wisdom
41. Type of tree
43. "No ___"
44. Rifts
46. Bridge positions
47. "It's ___ against time"
48. Director Rohmer
49. "The Lion King" lion
50. Heater stats
51. Manhattan's state: Abbr.
52. South American Indian
53. Great quantity
54. Daughter of Cronus
57. Circus cries

Puzzle 74

ACROSS
1. Metal
5. Wears out
10. Pain
14. "Salus populi suprema lex ___" (Missouri's motto)
15. Brightly coloured lizard
16. Ambition
17. Pert. to astigmatism
19. Subtle emanation
20. Pagans
21. Nasal
23. Gray of "Gray's Manual of Botany"
24. Combs et al.
25. Big name in fashion
29. Safety org.
30. Conductor ___-Pekka Salonen
33. Australian marsupial
34. Director Reiner
35. Precollege
36. "Wishing won't make ___"
37. Conceited
38. Run-down part of a city
39. Big name in magazine publishing
40. Exclamations of surprise
41. Make amends
42. Govt. agency that has your number
43. Upon
44. Thin
45. Meccan, e.g.
47. Sea (French)
48. Attractiveness
50. Lacking a face
55. Russia/Manchuria boundary river
56. Hawaii
58. Baltic capital
59. Alarm signal
60. Sketch
61. "Gil ___"
62. Stylish
63. Retired fleet

DOWN
1. Wife of Jacob
2. To be, to Brutus
3. Boy or girl lead-in
4. "I dare you!"
5. Son of Mary Stuart
6. Capital of Guam, old-style
7. Bygone auto
8. Brit. record label
9. Sacrosanctly
10. Encore
11. Adviser
12. ___-kiri
13. Airline to Israel
18. Republic in W Africa
22. Possessed
24. Chemises
25. Claude who starred in TV's "Lobo"
26. Duty rosters
27. Small rattlesnake
28. Buckets
29. Hairy-chested
31. Avoids
32. Anouk of "La Dolce Vita"
34. Raccoonlike carnivore
35. "Como ___ usted?"
37. Sissy
41. ___-ski
43. Not at home
44. Trig function
46. Subtle emanations
47. "Politically Incorrect" host
48. Point of hook
49. Disney's "___ and the Detectives"
50. ___ song
51. Former Fords
52. Hearing organs
53. Boxer's reach, e.g.
54. Stitches
57. Draw

Puzzle 75

ACROSS
1. Arm or leg
5. Lassoed
10. Certain herring
14. Musical direction
15. Nimble
16. Meat paste
17. Immeasurably deep
19. A Great Lake
20. More drowsy
21. Muscle contractions
23. Mail abbr.
24. Watch word
25. Noon
29. Judge's seat
30. Eavesdropping org.
33. Belief involving sorcery
34. Difficult
35. "How the Other Half Lives" author
36. "Happy Birthday, Moon" author Frank
37. Sharp pains
38. Puts on
39. 1994 Jodie Foster film
40. Mysterious symbol
41. Gravy
42. Simple fastener
43. Fly larvae
44. Short-legged dog
45. Italian wine
47. Speed up motor
48. Monopoly maker
50. Adorable
55. Et ___ (and others)
56. Historic mountain pass
58. Existence
59. Artist's stand
60. Blind as ___
61. States
62. Clothe
63. Soaks, as flax

DOWN
1. Bell ___
2. Image of a deity
3. Silent
4. Jean Renoir film "La ___ Humaine"
5. Extend into subdivisions
6. Leered
7. Jetty
8. 2002 British Open champion
9. Comes down
10. Talk
11. Melodious
12. Eagerly expectant
13. Odd couple?
18. Big name in book clubs
22. Rock's Ocasek
24. "Beetle Bailey" character
25. Haunted house sounds
26. Norwegian dramatist
27. Remove from security list
28. Author Roald
29. Notice of an intended marriage
31. From then on
32. Thing of value
34. High-toned
35. Vitamin bottle info
37. Brought on
41. Diligent banker of money
43. Metal rod
44. Inclines
46. Awards since 1956
47. Gowns
48. "The Laughing Cavalier" artist
49. Inter ___
50. Undergo lysis
51. On ___ with
52. Small child
53. Future atty.'s hurdle
54. Ballpark figs.
57. Kramden laugh syllable

150

Answer 1

P	A	C	E	D		B	L	A	B		S	T	A	G
R	O	U	T	E		R	E	M	Y		S	O	F	A
O	N	T	A	P		E	O	N	S		A	R	O	N
W	E	S	L	E	Y	A	N	I	S	M		T	U	E
			I	N	A		O	U	R	S	E	L	F	
E	C	H	I	D	N	A	S		S	I	L	L		
L	O	Y		S	K	U	L	K		S	O	L	A	N
K	I	P	S		S	E	E	R	S		B	I	D	E
O	R	E	A	D		R	E	I	N	A		N	A	E
	R	I	O	T		P	S	A	L	M	I	S	T	
T	I	S	S	U	E	S		I	K	E				
R	A	P		G	A	L	L	B	L	A	D	D	E	R
I	M	A	M		T	Y	P	E		L	I	E	T	O
A	B	C	D		E	E	G	S		I	C	E	A	X
L	I	E	S		D	R	A	T		S	I	S	S	Y

Answer 2

I	N	O	N	E		J	A	B	S		A	N	S	A
R	E	R	U	N		E	L	A	L		M	O	C	S
A	I	T	C	H		T	U	B	A		A	M	A	H
E	N	S	L	A	V	E	M	E	N	T		I	L	E
			E	N	A		S	T	R	A	N	D	S	
D	E	P	I	C	T	E	D		S	E	P	A		
O	R	R		E	I	D	E	R		S	E	T	A	E
E	M	E	R		C	H	I	C	K		R	I	M	A
R	A	D	O	N		S	C	A	L	A		V	A	S
	A	L	E	C		E	S	U	R	I	E	N	T	
U	N	C	L	E	A	N		T	E	N				
R	O	I		R	E	A	L	I	Z	A	T	I	O	N
B	R	O	S		S	C	A	B		W	I	L	L	A
A	G	U	A		A	R	M	A		A	M	I	E	S
N	E	S	T		R	E	A	R		Y	E	A	S	T

Answer 3

G	R	O	W	N		D	A	L	E		O	M	S	K
I	O	N	I	A		U	L	A	N		C	E	P	E
L	A	I	R	S		A	V	I	D		A	C	R	E
A	R	T	I	C	U	L	A	T	E	D		H	O	N
			N	E	B		Y	A	R	D	A	G	E	
D	I	A	G	N	O	S	E		R	E	I	N		
E	N	C		T	A	C	E	T		E	D	I	L	E
A	G	E	R		T	U	R	B	O		O	C	A	S
R	A	T	E	R		M	I	S	D	O		A	S	T
		I	N	E	S		E	P	I	S	T	L	E	S
R	E	C	O	A	T	S			S	T	E			
I	L	A		M	I	N	I	S	T	E	R	I	A	L
L	A	C	E		F	A	C	E		O	R	O	N	O
K	N	I	T		L	I	A	R		I	O	T	A	S
E	D	D	A		E	L	L	A		D	R	A	T	S

Answer 4

M	A	M	E	T		P	T	E	R		M	G	M	T
E	L	A	T	E		E	Y	R	E		I	L	E	A
C	I	T	E	S		E	P	I	C		N	I	T	S
H	E	A	R	T	B	R	O	K	E	N		T	A	T
			N	I	A		A	D	E	P	T	L	Y	
E	X	P	E	N	S	E	S		E	R	I	E		
D	E	O		G	I	L	L	S		O	K	R	A	S
E	R	N	E		C	I	A	O	S		E	A	R	N
N	O	D	A	L		E	B	B	E	D		T	I	E
		E	V	E	R		S	A	N	I	T	I	Z	E
F	O	R	E	S	E	E			S	N	A			
E	R	A		E	N	G	I	N	E	E	R	I	N	G
T	A	B	S		A	E	R	O		T	R	O	O	P
A	L	L	A		I	S	E	E		T	E	T	R	A
L	E	E	T		L	T	D	S		E	D	A	M	S

153

Answer 5

S	O	L	T	I		L	E	D	A		A	V	A	S
E	V	I	A	N		I	L	E	S		H	E	L	P
N	A	R	K	S		L	A	S	S		A	R	I	A
S	L	E	E	P	W	A	L	K	E	R		M	E	N
			T	E	E		S	N	A	K	I	N	G	
R	E	L	O	C	A	T	E		T	R	A	C		
O	M	A		T	R	U	C	E		A	K	E	R	S
S	I	C	K		S	M	O	C	K		A	L	O	W
E	L	E	N	A		S	L	O	A	N		L	A	I	
		R	E	C	T		E	L	B	O	W	I	N	G
P	R	A	E	T	O	R			O	T	O			
R	E	T		H	O	U	S	E	B	R	O	K	E	N
O	N	I	T		B	P	O	E		A	F	I	R	E
X	E	N	A		A	E	O	N		R	E	T	I	E
Y	E	G	G		D	E	N	Y		E	R	E	C	T

Answer 6

D	E	N	I	M		T	S	P	S		A	V	I	S
O	V	I	N	E		A	K	I	N		C	A	N	A
N	E	N	E	S		R	I	P	E		S	C	A	N
G	R	A	S	S	H	O	P	P	E	R		U	L	A
			S	I	E		A	R	U	G	U	L	A	
R	E	H	E	E	L	E	D		S	E	A	M		
I	M	A		R	E	P	A	Y		D	I	T	C	H
O	M	I	T		N	E	W	E	L		L	U	B	E
T	Y	R	E	S		E	E	L	E	D		B	E	N
		S	A	A	B		S	L	E	E	P	E	R	S
C	A	P	S	U	L	E			C	C	S			
O	R	R		L	E	V	E	L	H	E	A	D	E	D
R	A	I	L		N	I	L	E		A	L	U	L	A
A	C	N	E		D	A	B	S		S	M	E	L	T
L	E	G	O		S	N	E	E		E	S	S	E	S

Answer 7

T	I	P	S	Y		T	O	O	N		O	C	T	A
I	M	I	N	E		H	U	M	E		C	H	A	S
A	R	E	A	L		E	S	E	S		T	I	C	S
S	E	T	T	L	E	M	E	N	T	S		N	I	E
			C	I	D		S	E	L	E	C	T	S	
H	I	G	H	N	E	S	S		D	A	S	H		
E	N	A		G	N	O	M	E		B	A	I	L	S
A	T	T	N		S	A	U	C	E		U	L	A	N
D	R	E	A	D		K	S	T	A	R		L	Y	E
		K	L	E	E		H	O	M	E	B	A	S	E
B	R	E	A	S	T	S		E	U	R				
E	O	E		C	O	E	X	I	S	T	E	N	C	E
A	L	P	O		I	L	E	S		E	W	E	R	S
D	E	E	P		L	I	N	O		R	U	N	A	T
S	O	R	T		E	G	A	N		S	P	E	W	S

Answer 8

V	I	O	L	A		T	S	K	S		I	S	L	A
A	S	P	E	N		A	L	A	E		N	C	O	S
T	A	U	N	T		T	A	T	I		C	A	B	S
S	Y	S	T	E	M	A	T	I	Z	E		P	O	E
			E	N	E		E	E	R	I	E	S	T	
B	I	A	N	N	U	A	L		D	A	N	G		
O	T	C		A	S	K	E	W		S	E	R	A	C
N	A	T	S		E	I	G	E	R		S	A	N	A
E	L	I	H	U		N	U	T	S	O		C	I	R
		N	O	T	A		P	A	V	E	M	E	N	T
F	O	O	T	A	G	E			P	R	E			
I	L	L		H	A	R	N	E	S	S	R	A	C	E
N	E	I	N		M	O	O	T		T	I	R	E	S
K	A	T	E		I	D	E	A		E	N	O	L	S
S	N	E	E		C	E	L	L		D	O	W	S	E

154

Answer 9

L	T	G	E	N	░	M	U	S	E	░	O	D	I	E
O	R	I	B	I	░	A	P	A	R	░	N	E	O	N
M	E	L	B	A	░	L	A	R	A	░	O	L	D	S
A	S	T	I	G	M	A	T	I	S	M	░	I	O	U
░	N	A	Y	░	S	E	E	A	B	L	E			
R	I	B	G	R	A	S	S	░	D	O	M	E		
A	F	L	░	A	L	I	C	E	░	W	A	R	D	S
U	N	I	S	░	L	L	A	M	A	░	T	A	O	S
L	I	S	A	S	░	T	R	U	E	D	░	T	O	T
░	T	R	A	P	░	E	S	S	A	Y	E	R	S	
G	L	E	A	M	E	D	░	I	S	E				
S	I	R	░	P	O	R	T	E	R	H	O	U	S	E
T	A	I	L	░	P	A	R	S	░	E	M	M	E	T
A	N	N	I	░	L	I	A	M	░	R	A	B	A	T
R	A	G	S	░	E	N	D	E	░	S	N	O	R	E

Answer 10

B	O	N	E	S	░	S	C	U	D	░	A	D	O	S
U	R	A	N	O	░	A	A	R	E	░	D	E	K	E
S	C	R	U	M	░	B	I	A	S	░	S	A	A	R
S	A	C	R	A	M	E	N	T	A	L	░	C	P	I
░	E	L	Y	░	E	L	A	S	T	I	C			
M	I	S	S	I	L	E	S	░	T	O	P	I		
A	T	E	░	A	A	L	T	O	░	S	A	V	E	D
M	E	N	D	░	I	L	E	N	E	░	M	A	K	E
E	M	E	E	R	░	A	E	T	N	A	░	T	E	E
░	S	C	A	D	░	R	O	O	F	L	E	S	S	
I	N	C	I	S	E	D	░	C	F	O				
S	I	E	░	P	A	R	A	P	H	R	A	S	E	D
L	O	N	G	░	R	A	Z	E	░	O	F	A	G	E
A	B	C	S	░	M	C	A	T	░	N	E	R	O	S
M	E	E	T	░	E	O	N	S	░	T	R	I	N	I

Answer 11

P	L	E	A	D	░	R	D	A	S	░	C	S	T	
O	U	T	R	E	░	H	O	K	E	░	C	O	M	A
L	A	U	N	D	R	O	M	A	T	░	R	U	E	R
L	U	I	░	U	P	D	O	░	A	L	I	N	E	S
░	A	C	M	E	░	I	P	A	S	S				
F	E	A	S	T	S	░	S	N	A	P	P	E	R	S
R	O	U	T	S	░	S	L	U	R	P	░	L	E	E
O	S	S	A	░	A	P	A	R	T	░	A	L	V	A
R	I	T	░	A	M	I	N	E	░	P	R	O	E	M
E	N	R	A	G	I	N	G	░	P	E	A	R	L	S
░	A	U	N	T	S	░	C	U	R	L				
D	E	L	R	I	O	░	P	A	P	S	░	G	T	E
A	L	I	A	░	S	A	N	G	U	I	N	A	R	Y
W	E	A	L	░	I	S	E	E	░	S	E	G	U	E
N	A	N	░	S	P	U	D	░	T	W	E	E	D	

Answer 12

C	I	A	O	S	░	A	C	E	R	░	B	R	A	
L	A	R	R	Y	░	C	A	R	A	░	E	L	A	L
E	M	I	G	R	A	T	I	N	G	░	N	A	C	L
M	B	A	░	I	K	O	N	░	T	B	O	N	E	S
░	A	N	I	N	░	F	R	O	C	K				
M	A	L	I	G	N	░	P	O	A	C	H	E	R	S
C	L	A	R	E	░	G	O	L	D	A	░	T	E	N
G	O	B	Y	░	O	U	T	I	E	░	M	I	R	A
E	N	O	░	A	P	T	T	O	░	R	U	N	U	P
E	E	R	I	N	E	S	S	░	F	E	I	G	N	S
░	A	V	E	R	Y	░	P	I	E	R				
E	S	T	A	T	E	░	P	E	N	D	░	A	A	H
P	I	O	N	░	T	A	R	A	D	I	D	D	L	E
O	K	R	A	░	T	A	E	L	░	N	I	E	L	S
S	H	Y	░	A	S	P	S	░	G	R	E	A	T	

Answer 13

M	B	I	R	A	■	S	A	G	S	■	■	R	C	A
A	U	D	E	N	■	A	S	I	N	■	F	E	E	T
S	L	E	N	D	E	R	I	S	E	■	A	P	I	A
K	L	M	■	A	N	D	A	■	A	F	I	E	L	D
■	■	■	E	N	O	S	■	S	K	I	N	T	■	■
S	H	T	E	T	L	■	M	O	I	E	T	I	E	S
N	E	A	L	E	■	S	E	L	E	S	■	T	A	P
E	L	K	S	■	F	U	R	O	R	■	G	I	G	I
A	G	E	■	A	L	E	C	S	■	P	R	O	L	E
K	A	S	H	M	I	R	I	■	P	R	U	N	E	D
■	A	Y	E	R	S	■	D	R	I	B	■	■	■	■
I	N	D	E	N	T	■	S	H	O	E	■	A	B	M
F	A	I	N	■	I	M	P	O	S	S	I	B	L	E
S	I	V	A	■	N	E	A	L	■	T	A	R	A	S
O	R	E	■	G	A	M	E	■	S	M	A	S	H	■

Answer 14

M	O	S	E	S	■	S	M	U	G	■	■	F	A	T
O	V	A	R	Y	■	H	A	N	A	■	R	U	L	E
A	U	B	E	R	G	I	N	E	S	■	E	T	A	L
N	M	E	■	I	L	E	X	■	O	B	T	U	S	E
■	■	O	N	E	D	■	B	L	E	A	R	■	■	■
M	A	L	I	G	N	■	C	R	I	N	G	I	N	G
E	X	I	L	E	■	L	A	I	N	E	■	S	O	N
W	I	N	S	■	H	I	N	G	E	■	A	T	T	A
E	L	S	■	B	O	N	E	S	■	E	V	I	C	T
D	E	E	P	E	N	E	D	■	E	P	O	C	H	S
■	E	L	T	O	N	■	C	L	A	W	■	■	■	■
U	N	D	O	E	R	■	C	E	B	U	■	A	U	K
F	O	O	D	■	A	P	O	C	A	L	Y	P	S	E
O	T	I	S	■	N	O	R	I	■	E	A	S	E	L
S	E	L	■	D	I	A	L	■	T	H	O	R	P	■

Answer 15

U	N	P	E	N	■	P	R	A	M	■	R	A	S	■
H	A	R	T	E	■	I	A	G	O	■	B	E	R	T
U	N	I	C	A	M	E	R	A	L	■	A	C	M	E
H	O	G	■	R	O	T	A	■	E	R	N	E	S	T
■	D	E	L	A	■	S	C	U	D	S	■	■	■	■
E	N	D	U	S	E	■	T	H	U	M	B	S	U	P
B	E	R	E	T	■	C	O	I	L	S	■	I	N	I
O	R	A	L	■	C	A	R	N	E	■	B	O	T	S
A	D	M	■	F	O	C	U	S	■	C	A	N	I	T
T	S	A	R	I	N	A	S	■	F	O	C	S	L	E
■	T	A	X	C	O	■	S	I	N	H	■	■	■	■
P	R	I	M	E	R	■	O	L	A	F	■	B	E	A
H	A	S	P	■	E	X	C	I	T	E	M	E	N	T
A	C	T	S	■	T	E	A	M	■	C	O	R	O	T
T	E	S	■	E	R	S	E	■	T	O	I	L	S	■

Answer 16

M	E	D	E	A	■	A	S	T	A	■	■	Q	O	M
E	N	U	R	E	■	G	P	A	S	■	S	U	L	U
D	Y	S	A	R	T	H	R	I	A	■	T	E	E	S
S	O	T	■	A	W	A	Y	■	G	A	R	A	G	E
■	E	T	A	S	■	A	R	S	I	S	■	■	■	■
P	H	O	B	O	S	■	S	L	O	P	P	I	E	R
S	O	N	A	R	■	S	O	L	U	S	■	N	Y	E
A	L	E	N	■	A	T	R	I	P	■	M	E	R	E
L	E	A	■	S	C	R	E	E	■	L	A	S	I	K
M	Y	T	H	I	C	A	L	■	M	E	S	S	R	S
■	A	E	S	O	P	■	R	O	T	C	■	■	■	■
A	L	T	A	I	R	■	C	O	R	D	■	N	A	M
M	A	I	D	■	D	E	M	O	N	O	L	O	G	Y
A	T	M	S	■	E	X	O	D	■	W	I	D	E	N
H	E	E	■	D	E	N	S	■	N	A	I	R	A	■

Answer 17

S	O	B	E	R	█	S	H	A	H	█	█	P	S	S
P	H	A	S	E	█	C	Y	M	E	█	T	A	K	E
A	M	B	A	S	S	A	D	O	R	█	A	S	E	A
N	S	A	█	T	U	B	E	█	I	R	I	D	E	S
█	█	H	I	S	S	█	E	T	A	G	E	█	█	█
C	A	N	O	N	S	█	D	R	A	M	A	T	I	C
E	W	I	N	G	█	B	R	A	G	S	█	R	N	A
S	A	T	E	█	A	L	A	T	E	█	N	O	O	N
A	R	P	█	A	M	I	N	O	█	C	A	I	N	E
R	E	I	G	N	I	N	G	█	D	A	I	S	E	S
█	█	C	L	A	C	K	█	L	A	R	F	█	█	█
D	A	K	O	T	A	█	G	E	N	A	█	B	O	D
A	P	I	A	█	B	L	A	C	K	B	E	R	R	Y
C	A	N	T	█	L	I	S	I	█	A	L	O	N	E
E	R	G	█	█	E	S	T	D	█	O	O	Z	E	D

Answer 18

S	T	O	N	E	█	A	S	O	K	█	█	K	A	I
C	A	V	I	L	█	S	O	R	E	█	S	I	L	L
A	L	I	M	E	N	T	A	R	Y	█	N	D	A	K
D	I	D	█	V	E	E	S	█	S	P	I	N	E	S
█	█	W	E	A	R	█	U	T	I	C	A	█	█	█
W	I	S	E	N	T	█	C	R	O	C	K	P	O	T
I	D	E	A	S	█	A	L	A	N	A	█	P	R	O
S	A	N	K	█	E	M	O	T	E	█	B	E	A	T
E	H	S	█	B	R	I	D	E	█	G	I	R	L	S
S	O	U	L	L	E	S	S	█	F	L	O	S	S	Y
█	A	H	E	M	S	█	F	L	A	G	█	█	█	█
M	A	L	A	W	I	█	C	U	E	D	█	M	A	G
A	C	I	S	█	T	H	R	E	A	D	B	A	R	E
G	A	Z	A	█	E	M	I	L	█	E	O	S	I	N
E	D	E	█	█	S	O	B	S	█	N	A	S	A	L

Answer 19

B	E	R	E	A	█	C	H	A	D	█	█	A	A	S
O	R	A	L	S	█	L	E	T	O	█	C	C	C	P
S	N	U	F	F	B	O	X	E	S	█	A	T	T	A
H	E	L	█	A	I	D	A	█	S	A	D	I	E	S
█	█	A	R	C	S	█	R	I	P	E	N	█	█	█
P	A	S	H	A	S	█	M	A	E	S	T	O	S	O
E	S	T	A	S	█	F	E	R	R	O	█	L	Y	S
R	I	A	S	█	L	O	R	E	S	█	K	I	R	I
E	D	T	█	A	I	S	L	E	█	S	A	T	I	E
S	E	E	D	C	A	S	E	█	L	I	N	E	A	R
█	C	E	L	I	A	█	B	E	T	A	█	█	█	█
A	I	R	B	U	S	█	P	E	A	U	█	S	D	I
A	L	A	I	█	I	N	T	E	R	A	C	T	E	D
H	E	F	T	█	N	E	E	R	█	T	E	A	S	E
S	A	T	█	█	G	O	R	Y	█	E	N	N	I	S

Answer 20

F	L	O	C	K	█	T	A	I	N	T	█	C	E	L
I	O	N	I	A	█	E	L	M	E	R	█	O	L	E
S	C	I	N	T	I	L	L	A	T	E	█	N	I	T
H	I	T	E	█	N	E	I	G	H	█	N	C	A	A
█	█	M	I	N	G	█	E	E	R	I	E	S	T	█
D	E	B	A	T	E	R	S	█	R	A	G	A	█	█
I	R	A	█	E	R	A	T	O	█	M	E	L	B	A
V	A	C	A	█	S	M	O	L	T	█	R	I	P	S
A	S	K	E	D	█	S	M	E	A	R	█	N	O	I
█	G	R	U	B	█	A	C	R	E	A	G	E	S	█
A	F	R	I	C	A	N	█	R	O	A	D	█	█	█
A	L	O	E	█	R	E	S	A	T	█	D	A	I	S
L	E	U	█	B	R	A	I	N	S	T	O	R	M	S
T	E	N	█	R	E	P	R	O	█	S	N	O	R	T
O	R	D	█	O	L	S	E	N	█	E	S	N	E	S

Answer 21

```
B E A R S   ■ S O R E N ■   T S P
L U R E D   ■ U K A S E ■   O P E
O R I G I N A L I T Y ■   R E A
T O L E ■ I V A N A ■ E T A L
■ A C H E ■ S T A Y E R S
U N E R R I N G ■ E A R L ■
M A C ■ I L E A C ■ A I L E D
P H O S ■ O S L E R ■ E I N E
S A N A A ■ S A M O S ■ N E B
■ O M N I ■ H E D O N I S T
A R M B A N D ■ N E N E ■
G A I A ■ T O N T O ■ G O U T
O T C ■ R E N A I S S A N C E
R I A ■ A N N A N ■ A T A L L
A O L ■ S T A N G ■ P E N A L
```

Answer 22

```
N O M A N ■ T I T H E ■ C M A
E N E M A ■ E L R O Y ■ A I M
R E N E G O T I A T E ■ N N E
D R U B ■ B R A I D ■ I N O N
■ I O L A ■ L O A D E R S
T R U C K A G E ■ G U L L ■
R O N ■ A T R I A ■ G E L I D
I T E M ■ E A G E R ■ D O M E
M I M E R ■ M E R E S ■ N S A
■ P R E P ■ R O T A T I O N
P U L L T A B ■ L O M A ■
S L O E ■ R E A I R ■ U P D O
A N Y ■ S A G I T T A R I U S
L A E ■ A D O R E ■ P U C K S
M E D ■ P E T E S ■ O S S E O
```

Answer 23

```
R E E F S ■ T R E A D ■ O S T
E L C I D ■ H I L L Y ■ M T A
C E R T I F I C A T E ■ N A B
T A U T ■ U R A T E ■ D I D O
■ E S T D ■ E R N E S T O
A P E R T U R E ■ S N C C ■
M A A ■ U R A L S ■ E K I N G
E G G S ■ A T E A T ■ S E E R
R E L I C ■ E N D U E ■ N A E
■ E X I T ■ A D R O I T L Y
I N S T O R E ■ E N E S ■
R A C Y ■ I N A N E ■ R I A S
A M O ■ F O R B I D D A N C E
N E U ■ A D O R N ■ H E F T S
I S T ■ S E L I G ■ S L O E S
```

Answer 24

```
N E A T H ■ D R A F T ■ D S C
I S L A M ■ R I P E R ■ H U H
T E M P O R A L I T Y ■ A L I
A S A P ■ E C L A T ■ A U L D
■ E R G O ■ N E B U L A E
H E A D B A N D ■ R U G A ■
A R B ■ I L I A C ■ M E G A N
M D S E ■ E A R L S ■ R I D E
S A T Y R ■ N I E C E ■ R E B
■ E D I T ■ O R R E R I E S
C O M I C A L ■ G E N E ■
I L I E ■ T O N Y A ■ N E S S
R O O ■ R E C O M M E N D E D
C R U ■ A R O M A ■ M E D E A
E D S ■ E S S E N ■ S T A N K
```

Answer 25

Answer 26

Answer 27

Answer 28

Answer 29

H	A	R	P	S	■	B	A	N	G	S	■	■	S	A	T
A	R	D	E	N	■	E	C	O	L	E	■	■	A	X	E
A	C	A	T	A	L	E	C	T	I	C	■	■	N	I	X
G	A	S	T	■	O	F	T	E	N	■	■	L	A	N	A
▬	▬	▬	■	E	I	N	E	■	S	T	R	I	N	G	S
S	E	E	D	L	E	A	F	■	■	S	E	A	T	■	■
I	N	N	■	A	R	T	I	E	■	S	N	O	B	S	■
E	D	U	C	■	S	E	T	U	P	■	G	N	A	T	■
G	E	N	R	E	■	R	I	C	A	N	■	I	R	E	■
■	■	C	I	N	Q	■	N	A	P	I	F	O	R	M	■
A	T	I	S	S	U	E	■	L	E	T	O	■	■	■	■
S	O	A	P	■	A	S	S	Y	R	■	R	A	R	A	■
S	I	T	■	A	N	T	I	P	Y	R	E	T	I	C	■
A	L	E	■	A	G	E	N	T	■	O	G	I	V	E	■
M	E	S	■	H	O	R	N	S	■	T	O	P	E	R	■

Answer 30

S	C	A	B	■	S	E	N	A	T	■	■	P	A	A	R
P	U	M	A	■	A	L	I	C	E	■	■	E	S	S	E
E	B	B	S	■	N	I	C	H	E	■	■	D	I	C	E
L	I	L	A	C	S	■	H	O	U	D	I	N	I	■	■
T	C	E	L	L	▬	▬	T	O	P	I	C	■	■	■	■
■	■	■	T	U	B	A	■	■	O	U	N	C	E	■	■
G	R	R	■	B	A	R	R	I	E	R	R	E	E	F	■
R	I	O	T	■	L	U	A	N	N	■	E	A	S	T	■
E	M	B	A	N	K	M	E	N	T	S	■	P	S	S	■
G	A	B	B	Y	■	■	S	R	I	S	■	■	■	■	■
■	■	L	E	N	T	O	■	R	H	E	A	S	■	■	■
P	O	E	T	E	S	S	■	P	S	E	U	D	O	■	■
P	U	P	A	■	A	L	C	O	A	■	I	L	L	Y	■
F	R	A	U	■	T	O	A	S	T	■	L	E	I	A	■
C	A	L	X	■	S	T	R	O	H	■	A	R	B	S	■

Answer 31

B	O	C	A	■	A	C	I	N	G	■	I	C	B	M
L	I	L	I	■	T	I	M	O	R	■	N	A	O	S
E	L	A	L	■	M	E	A	R	A	■	F	I	N	N
A	E	R	I	E	S	■	M	I	N	C	I	N	G	■
K	R	O	N	A	■	S	A	T	I	N	■	■	■	■
■	■	G	R	O	K	■	■	A	I	D	E	S	■	■
A	D	M	■	P	L	E	N	I	P	O	T	E	N	T
M	O	E	T	■	A	P	A	S	T	■	E	E	N	Y
T	I	G	H	T	F	I	S	T	E	D	■	S	A	E
S	T	A	I	R	■	■	S	R	I	S	■	■	■	■
■	■	■	N	E	P	A	L	■	O	P	R	A	H	■
M	O	N	T	A	G	E	■	G	R	O	Y	N	E	■
B	O	R	E	■	B	R	A	C	E	■	I	D	E	M
R	U	B	S	■	L	I	K	E	S	■	L	E	M	A
R	E	S	T	■	O	N	S	E	T	■	T	R	O	N

Answer 32

L	I	D	O	■	B	A	S	T	E	■	M	S	G	R
T	N	U	T	■	A	C	H	E	S	■	A	H	A	B
C	O	L	T	■	S	H	E	E	T	■	N	A	Z	I
O	N	S	E	T	S	■	I	N	A	R	A	G	E	■
L	E	E	R	S	■	K	A	B	U	L	■	■	■	■
■	■	■	S	A	A	B	■	■	H	I	D	E	S	■
N	A	S	■	R	O	O	M	S	E	R	V	I	C	E
A	L	O	E	■	K	O	T	O	W	■	E	R	O	S
C	A	F	F	E	I	N	A	T	E	D	■	E	N	S
L	E	A	F	S	■	■	O	R	E	L	■	■	■	■
■	■	■	I	T	E	M	S	■	N	E	A	L	E	■
N	I	G	E	R	I	A	■	S	T	A	G	E	R	■
D	E	S	I	■	R	A	R	E	E	■	D	O	D	O
A	D	U	E	■	O	M	E	G	A	■	E	G	I	S
T	S	P	S	■	L	I	E	O	N	■	D	O	N	E

Answer 33

Answer 34

K	I	T	T			C	A	C	A	O			L	A	I	R
E	R	I	E			O	V	O	L	O			O	U	S	E
A	I	L	S			L	A	R	C	H			O	D	I	C
T	S	E	T	S	E			D	O	E	S	K	I	N		
S	H	R	E	D				S	A	D	H	U				
			D	A	D	A				E	P	O	D	E		
H	O	G			K	I	L	O	C	A	L	O	R	I	E	
I	K	E	A		A	L	T	O	N			N	I	C	K	
P	R	O	S	E	L	Y	T	I	S	M			G	E	S	
S	A	L	I	C				N	A	U	T					
			S	U	G	A	R				O	R	A	L	E	
	T	R	E	A	C	L	E			S	N	O	R	E	S	
G	I	B	E			L	O	P	P	Y			P	I	O	N
A	L	I	I			E	N	I	A	C			P	O	N	E
L	E	S	T			F	E	N	C	E			O	T	I	S

Answer 35

Answer 36

F	A	C	E			T	E	S	S	A			D	O	O	R
E	N	E	S			I	C	T	U	S			E	A	R	N
E	G	I	S			C	O	A	S	T			R	H	E	A
L	I	B	E	L	S			R	H	O	D	I	U	M		
S	E	A	N	S				K	I	R	O	V				
			E	A	C	H				H	A	L	L	S		
A	H	A			T	R	A	N	S	L	A	T	I	O	N	
J	I	L	T			A	K	I	T	A			E	S	S	E
A	L	P	H	A	B	E	T	I	Z	E			A	T	E	
R	O	S	E	N				R	Y	E	S					
			A	N	N	A	S				G	L	A	C	E	
	C	O	R	S	A	G	E			I	S	O	B	A	R	
N	A	R	C			D	O	D	O	S			G	I	G	I
P	T	A	H			I	N	E	R	T			A	D	E	E
R	E	L	Y			A	Y	R	E	S			N	E	D	S

Answer 37

I	A	G	O	■	M	A	L	T	A	■	D	E	N	E
M	E	O	W	■	A	T	H	O	S	■	I	P	O	D
A	R	O	N	■	S	M	A	R	T	■	S	I	G	H
M	I	S	E	R	S	■	S	I	R	O	C	C	O	■
S	E	E	R	S	■	A	I	O	L	I	■	■	■	■
■	■	■	S	V	E	N	■	■	E	P	E	E	S	
I	N	D	■	P	L	A	N	E	T	O	L	O	G	Y
C	O	O	N	■	A	V	I	L	A	■	E	N	O	S
B	R	O	O	K	L	Y	N	E	S	E	■	S	S	T
M	A	M	B	A	■	■	A	S	S	T	■			
■	■	I	L	I	A	C	■	T	I	L	E	D		
■	S	A	L	E	R	N	O	■	M	A	N	A	N	A
A	N	T	I	■	R	E	N	E	E	■	K	N	O	W
R	I	T	T	■	E	L	A	N	D	■	E	A	R	N
I	T	S	Y	■	G	E	N	E	S	■	R	I	M	S

Answer 38

R	P	M	S	■	E	N	O	L	A	■	B	A	T	E
O	R	E	O	■	S	O	L	E	D	■	E	U	R	O
I	M	A	M	■	T	I	D	A	L	■	A	D	O	S
L	A	R	E	D	O	■	I	N	A	S	N	I	T	■
S	N	A	R	E	■	E	N	I	A	C	■	■	■	■
■	■	■	S	L	E	D	■	■	D	U	B	A	I	
P	B	S	■	A	B	E	C	E	D	A	R	I	A	N
I	L	E	A	■	A	B	A	C	O	■	D	O	H	S
M	A	G	N	A	N	I	M	O	U	S	■	G	S	T
A	S	A	H	I	■	■	L	P	G	A	■			
■	■	E	R	S	E	S	■	T	I	A	R	A		
■	S	Q	U	E	L	C	H	■	A	S	L	E	E	P
T	A	U	S	■	A	L	A	N	A	■	I	S	A	R
I	R	A	E	■	G	A	P	E	R	■	N	I	T	E
P	A	I	R	■	S	T	E	E	P	■	G	R	A	S

Answer 39

M	E	N	D	■	B	I	F	I	D	■	T	R	I	S
A	N	Y	A	■	A	D	E	N	O	■	A	A	R	E
D	O	M	S	■	M	A	I	D	S	■	I	N	A	S
A	L	P	H	A	S	■	G	R	E	M	L	I	N	■
M	A	H	E	R	■	N	A	D	I	R	■	■	■	■
■	■	■	R	I	T	E	■	N	A	A	C	P		
R	I	B	■	L	O	G	I	S	T	I	C	I	A	N
I	O	L	A	■	M	A	S	E	R	■	E	R	N	E
S	W	E	L	L	E	D	H	E	A	D	■	E	A	U
K	A	D	A	I	■	D	Y	A	D	■	■	■		
■	C	E	N	S	E	■	B	R	A	H	E			
■	T	R	A	D	E	O	N	■	A	S	I	D	E	S
M	O	O	R	■	R	O	G	E	T	■	E	L	L	S
S	C	U	T	■	O	T	E	R	O	■	S	E	L	A
S	K	E	E	■	S	H	L	E	P	■	T	R	O	Y

Answer 40

F	A	B	L	E	■	I	P	A	S	S	■	M	A	A
O	W	L	E	T	■	N	E	W	E	L	■	A	P	P
A	N	T	E	C	E	D	E	N	C	E	■	N	A	S
M	S	S	■	H	A	I	R	■	T	E	N	U	R	E
■	■	L	I	S	A	■	C	O	P	E	S	■		
B	E	G	O	N	E	■	F	A	R	O	U	C	H	E
R	E	R	I	G	■	L	O	D	E	N	■	R	A	I
A	L	E	N	■	G	O	U	R	D	■	G	I	L	D
K	E	G	■	S	O	C	L	E	■	M	A	P	L	E
E	D	A	C	I	O	U	S	■	D	E	B	T	O	R
■	R	I	N	D	S	■	S	U	M	S	■			
S	K	I	R	U	N	■	M	U	T	E	■	S	H	O
C	O	O	■	A	E	R	O	D	Y	N	A	M	I	C
A	B	U	■	T	S	A	R	S	■	T	R	U	T	H
D	E	S	■	E	S	S	A	Y	■	O	A	T	E	S

Answer 41

F	E	E	D	S	■	A	T	T	A	R	■	S	S	A
A	K	E	L	A	■	L	E	A	S	E	■	T	K	O
C	E	L	E	S	T	I	A	L	L	Y	■	E	I	N
T	D	S	■	S	A	A	R	■	O	N	T	A	P	E
■	■	S	I	T	S	■	G	N	A	R	L	■	■	
P	E	E	W	E	E	■	A	I	G	R	E	T	T	E
E	R	R	O	R	■	I	N	B	A	D	■	H	A	D
A	N	A	T	■	A	N	T	E	S	■	M	I	T	A
R	I	D	■	D	E	L	E	S	■	G	O	L	E	M
L	E	I	S	U	R	E	D	■	S	A	T	Y	R	S
■	C	O	R	O	T	■	S	I	Z	E	■	■		
S	T	A	L	A	G	■	L	O	D	E	■	E	S	P
L	O	B	■	B	R	A	I	N	S	T	O	R	M	S
A	T	L	■	L	A	B	A	N	■	T	O	L	E	T
B	E	E	■	E	M	E	R	Y	■	E	P	E	E	S

Answer 42

B	R	I	A	R	■	O	D	O	R	S	■	E	C	O
E	A	R	L	E	■	L	I	T	H	E	■	L	A	C
L	I	M	P	W	R	I	S	T	E	D	■	E	F	T
S	N	A	■	R	O	O	K	■	O	U	N	C	E	S
■	■	D	I	O	S	■	A	S	C	O	T	■		
A	B	B	O	T	S	■	I	N	T	E	G	R	A	L
S	L	O	P	E	■	O	C	T	A	D	■	I	B	O
S	A	T	E	■	Q	U	I	E	T	■	S	C	O	W
N	I	T	■	O	U	T	E	D	■	M	E	A	D	E
S	N	O	O	P	I	E	R	■	C	U	R	L	E	D
■	M	I	S	E	R	■	B	A	T	S	■	■		
B	A	L	L	O	T	■	I	L	E	A	■	J	A	G
I	C	E	■	N	U	R	S	I	N	G	H	O	M	E
A	H	S	■	I	D	O	L	S	■	E	M	A	I	L
S	E	S	■	N	E	N	E	S	■	N	O	N	E	T

Answer 43

D	O	E	R	S	■	O	B	E	A	H	■	S	M	A
A	T	R	I	P	■	H	A	V	E	A	■	T	E	L
B	O	L	D	A	S	B	R	A	S	S	■	R	I	A
S	S	E	■	R	O	O	K	■	O	S	C	A	R	S
■	■	O	R	L	Y	■	S	P	L	A	T	■		
H	O	O	D	O	O	■	A	L	I	E	N	A	T	E
E	L	B	O	W	■	S	T	E	A	D	■	G	R	R
S	E	J	M	■	K	A	R	E	N	■	R	E	I	N
S	I	E	■	M	E	R	I	T	■	C	O	M	B	S
E	C	C	L	E	S	I	A	■	P	R	E	S	E	T
■	T	E	N	T	S	■	H	A	A	G	■	■		
A	M	I	N	O	R	■	C	E	R	F	■	L	A	P
C	A	V	■	R	E	G	U	L	A	T	I	O	N	S
T	H	E	■	C	L	A	R	E	■	E	N	N	I	S
S	I	S	■	A	S	P	E	N	■	D	O	E	S	T

Answer 44

M	I	L	E	S	■	E	G	E	S	T	■	D	T	S
M	B	I	R	A	■	L	E	V	E	E	■	E	O	E
M	I	S	E	R	L	I	N	E	S	S	■	S	P	A
M	S	T	■	C	O	A	L	■	S	T	O	P	I	N
■	■	H	O	P	S	■	T	I	A	R	A	■		
D	A	S	S	I	E	■	S	H	O	C	K	I	N	G
F	L	U	I	D	■	S	P	I	N	Y	■	R	A	E
L	A	M	A	■	C	A	R	E	S	■	R	I	M	E
A	T	M	■	S	H	E	A	F	■	B	O	N	E	S
T	E	E	T	H	I	N	G	■	A	L	E	G	R	E
■	R	E	A	M	S	■	S	I	E	G	■	■		
R	A	C	E	M	E	■	L	T	D	S	■	T	A	I
I	L	A	■	A	R	B	O	R	E	S	C	E	N	T
N	I	M	■	N	I	O	B	E	■	E	S	T	E	S
K	I	P	■	S	C	O	O	P	■	S	A	R	T	O

Answer 45

Answer 46

Answer 47

Answer 48

Answer 49

```
S A B E R . S E A R . S E A L
E M I L E . E L L E . A N D A
A B R O G A T I O N . S D A K
M O O . E N S A T E . H O P E
. . A N T I . G I A N T S . .
P E N I T E N T I A R Y . . .
A V E R S . A D D S . D A L .
P E A S . A L B E E . B Y T E
A R T . B R I O . S A N T O .
. . P R O P R I E T R E S S .
A G L E A M . B A A S . . . .
C R U E . A G L E T S . B I S
M A R V . T E A R S H E E T S
E P E E . I N T I . E C L A T
S E S S . C A S A . D O L L S
```

Answer 50

```
P R E E N . C A L M . D E E M
O U T D O . I L E A . I N C A
R E N O V A T I O N . G R O G
N R A . E R R A N D . G O L D
. . A L T O . A M E L I A . .
S H O O T I N G S T A R . . .
P I C K Y . R A E S . M O C .
A L A I . M O U L D . M O N A
S T S . F A R M . T E A C H .
. . K I N D E R G A R T E N .
A M O E B A . E A R L . . . .
N I P A . C H A F E S . D D E
K N I T . L O C A L I T I E S
L E N O . E R I C . E A M E S
E D E N . S A S E . R U S S E
```

Answer 51

```
A O R T A . N E A P . G A P S
L E A D S . A G N I . A C R E
D I S S E C T I N G . M O O G
A L P . P L U S E S . B R N O
. . S T A R . T B O N E S . .
P R O V I D E N T I A L . . .
R E B E C . G A E L . A C S .
A N I N . C H A O S . B A M A
T A T . N A S I . C A R D S .
. . T E E T O T A L L E R S .
A D I E U S . A T O M . . . .
C A N A . A D A P T S . B A H
C L U B . R E G E N E R A C Y
T A R A . E M E R . S I D E D
S I N G . A I R S . T A S S E
```

Answer 52

```
S N O O T . S A M P . I C A L
O A K I E . N O O R . O O N A
I N E L E G A N C E . D A I S
L A Y . P R I E S T . A C M E
. . R E A L . E I T H E R . .
H A P P E N S T A N C E . . .
E X A M S . E A C H . H A M .
R E P S . A B A S E . C O N G
R R S . O T I C . P A N A M .
. . P S Y C H O L O G I S T .
M I S H A P . N I L E . . . .
I C K Y . I N E S S E . S E I
D I E S . C A D E T C O R P S
A L I I . A M A T . A R T I E
S Y N C . L E M S . T E A S E
```

Answer 53

K	I	O	S	K	▪	S	P	A	S	▪	C	A	M	E
O	D	O	U	R	▪	A	R	I	A	▪	A	B	E	L
P	E	P	P	E	R	C	O	R	N	▪	N	E	A	L
H	A	S	▪	M	E	R	G	E	D	▪	T	A	L	I
▪	▪	▪	E	L	E	A	▪	▪	L	H	O	T	S	E
F	I	B	R	I	L	L	A	T	I	O	N	▪	▪	▪
A	C	O	R	N	▪	▪	L	A	K	E	▪	P	E	I
C	O	D	S	▪	R	I	F	L	E	▪	B	A	S	T
E	N	E	▪	N	O	R	I	▪	P	E	L	T	S	▪
▪	▪	▪	C	H	O	R	E	O	G	R	A	P	H	Y
I	T	S	E	L	F	▪	M	E	E	K	▪	▪	▪	▪
P	A	C	A	▪	L	I	N	E	A	L	▪	S	A	S
A	N	A	S	▪	E	M	I	G	R	A	T	I	N	G
S	I	N	E	▪	S	R	T	A	▪	T	A	R	O	T
S	A	S	S	▪	S	E	S	S	▪	E	V	E	N	S

Answer 54

B	R	A	C	E	▪	O	T	I	S	▪	B	A	R	A
L	I	E	O	N	▪	L	A	R	A	▪	O	W	E	D
A	G	R	E	A	T	D	E	A	L	▪	R	A	I	D
S	A	Y	▪	C	A	P	L	E	T	▪	E	R	N	E
▪	▪	▪	S	T	I	R	▪	▪	L	E	A	D	E	D
B	A	C	H	E	L	O	R	G	I	R	L	▪	▪	▪
P	S	E	U	D	▪	▪	O	R	C	A	▪	C	A	M
O	I	S	E	▪	C	H	I	R	K	▪	H	O	T	E
E	A	T	▪	D	H	A	L	▪	▪	S	E	R	T	A
▪	▪	▪	R	E	A	S	S	I	G	N	M	E	N	T
S	A	L	A	M	I	▪	▪	C	E	E	S	▪	▪	▪
A	L	A	I	▪	R	E	C	I	T	E	▪	F	R	A
B	I	R	L	▪	M	Y	O	C	A	R	D	I	U	M
I	N	G	E	▪	A	R	I	L	▪	A	L	L	I	E
N	E	E	D	▪	N	E	N	E	▪	T	E	E	N	S

Answer 55

C	O	D	E	S	▪	A	F	A	R	▪	F	A	L	A
A	G	A	N	A	▪	S	O	R	E	▪	I	C	E	S
N	E	T	T	L	E	S	O	M	E	▪	N	U	N	S
S	E	A	▪	E	L	I	D	E	D	▪	I	T	I	N
▪	▪	▪	D	R	E	G	▪	P	A	T	E	N	S	▪
A	N	T	A	N	A	N	A	R	I	V	O	▪	▪	▪
T	A	E	B	O	▪	▪	R	O	P	E	▪	G	E	S
M	B	A	S	▪	E	L	I	T	E	▪	B	I	T	E
S	S	T	▪	A	R	E	A	▪	▪	S	E	R	T	A
▪	▪	▪	I	N	A	U	S	P	I	C	I	O	U	S
R	E	I	N	A	S	▪	▪	I	R	O	N	▪	▪	▪
I	N	S	T	▪	A	R	M	P	I	T	▪	E	C	O
C	A	S	E	▪	B	O	O	K	S	E	L	L	E	R
I	T	E	R	▪	L	O	R	I	▪	R	E	S	I	N
N	E	I	N	▪	E	T	O	N	▪	S	T	A	L	E

Answer 56

E	L	S	I	E	▪	A	C	M	E	▪	S	A	M	E
R	O	L	L	S	▪	C	O	O	N	▪	E	M	I	L
I	D	I	O	P	A	T	H	I	C	▪	C	A	L	I
N	E	T	▪	O	R	I	O	L	E	▪	E	T	A	S
▪	▪	▪	A	U	T	O	▪	▪	I	O	D	I	N	E
J	A	I	L	S	E	N	T	E	N	C	E	▪	▪	▪
A	B	O	V	E	▪	▪	A	C	T	H	▪	L	I	B
P	E	N	A	▪	C	A	R	T	E	▪	P	I	S	A
E	D	S	▪	C	H	A	D	▪	▪	M	I	L	E	R
▪	▪	▪	L	O	O	S	E	J	O	I	N	T	E	D
S	A	F	A	R	I	▪	▪	A	N	N	A	▪	▪	▪
O	D	I	C	▪	C	A	D	M	U	S	▪	F	D	A
A	M	O	K	▪	E	Q	U	E	S	T	R	I	A	N
M	A	R	E	▪	S	U	E	S	▪	E	N	A	M	I
I	N	D	Y	▪	T	A	T	I	▪	R	A	T	E	L

Answer 57

Answer 58

Answer 59

Answer 60

Answer 61

```
DROP ■ DACCA ■ RIAS
AURA  INLET ■ EDDA
BLACKDEATH ■ DEED
SENILITY ■ ESSENE
■ FIN ■ SNEE ■
■ MEIN ■ ERIECANAL
SENSE ■ GAMUT ■ EGO
ATOM ■ GRIMM ■ ERGS
GAL ■ MEESE ■ OLDIE
ALABASTER ■ RAYE ■
■ AMTS ■ AMP ■
LANDAU ■ MOLESKIN
OBOE ■ REPATRIATE
BURG ■ ERATO ■ NYSE
STAG ■ SLAYS ■ GOOD
```

Answer 62

```
UGHS ■ BLABS ■ LONG
CATT ■ RESEE ■ ASEA
ALTOGETHER ■ AHAB
LAPUENTE ■ VAGARY
■ TAS ■ MIME ■
■ APER ■ DEUTERIUM
AMASS ■ ENSOR ■ NNE
CIST ■ NADIR ■ TEDS
TSE ■ SALON ■ TORUS
ISOLATING ■ HOTE
■ IRAN ■ GUT ■
DEFEAT ■ AMIDSHIP
SLUG ■ IMPASSIONS
OISE ■ OPIUM ■ EDIT
SASS ■ NGAIO ■ SSTS
```

Answer 63

```
EARL ■ PHONO ■ APAR
EDIE ■ HELEN ■ RODE
LAVATORIES ■ MEAL
SHERATON ■ CLAMMY
■ NCO ■ BRED ■
■ PEEK ■ AGREEABLE
MYERS ■ PLIER ■ OAK
ALLS ■ LEANN ■ BINE
COE ■ PIXIE ■ BASKS
ENDANGERS ■ OBEY
■ BEAS ■ COY ■
INDIUM ■ SLATTING
DUAD ■ ENCEPHALON
ELLE ■ NEATO ■ LEIA
SLED ■ TAGON ■ KART
```

Answer 64

```
ASSN ■ EBOLA ■ HERA
PUPU ■ LOMAN ■ OTIS
PLUTOCRACY ■ HUTT
LUNARIAN ■ TAHITI
■ TAD ■ SHMO ■
■ NOIL ■ SATIATING
DEFOE ■ PEENS ■ SUE
EGAN ■ RERIG ■ NILS
KEG ■ SEEIN ■ DEALT
EVENTIDES ■ OOHS
■ EONS ■ RON ■
SHREWD ■ EGOMANIA
LAUD ■ ENTRUSTING
ALIT ■ ENNIS ■ ATKA
BONO ■ READE ■ LASS
```

Answer 65

```
I M I T ■ I M A M S ■ S S T S
C O M A ■ S A L S A ■ C H A T
E M A C I A T I N G ■ R O D E
L A M I N A T E ■ A B A D A N
■ T A C ■ S C O W ■ ■ ■
■ R A U L ■ C O T I L L I O N
C H U R L ■ A L A T E ■ N R A
H O R N ■ B U M P Y ■ S T E P
A D A ■ B A S E L ■ A U R A E
R E L A Y R A C E ■ A P O D ■
■ F E E L ■ A R E ■ ■
P A R I S H ■ M E M O R I S E
A D E E ■ E L I M I N A T E D
G E N L ■ A I L E D ■ D E L A
E S T D ■ D E E R E ■ D R A M
```

Answer 66

```
M E A D ■ D E A L S ■ O C A S
U N T O ■ E R G O T ■ R O L E
N E I G H B O R L Y ■ P H A R
I S T H A T S O ■ L A H O R E
■ O N S ■ P U M A ■ ■
■ S P U D ■ P A R S O N A G E
A M E S S ■ E P E E S ■ S U D
M E R E ■ C A R T S ■ O K R A
E L K ■ L I C I T ■ O D E U M
S T Y L I S H L Y ■ C O W S ■
■ A L L Y ■ T A M ■ ■
N A S S A U ■ O M E L E T T E
A B U T ■ N O M I N A T I N G
P A L E ■ A M E N D ■ E T U I
S T U D ■ R A N K S ■ R O T S
```

Answer 67

```
L E A P ■ E A S E R ■ M A M E
O T T O ■ S C A R E ■ O P E R
A T T E M P T I N G ■ C P A S
D E N T U R E S ■ I N H A L E
■ S I D ■ G S T A R ■ ■
R A B B E T ■ S E T H ■ I L L
O A R E D ■ C H A R ■ S T O L
A L O E ■ C L A R Y ■ M I R O
C T N S ■ O A K S ■ P E O N Y
H O T ■ H O M E ■ M A E N A D
■ O R A L S ■ K E W ■ ■
E A S E I N ■ A R E A C O D E
A L A E ■ E M B I T T E R E D
S T U D ■ S T A L L ■ C A S H
E A R S ■ S A D L Y ■ E L I S
```

Answer 68

```
S I B S ■ D R A C O ■ S H A D
E D E N ■ E E L E R ■ N O I R
A L L E G A T I O N ■ E R D A
L E G E N D R E ■ I M A R E T
■ O E O ■ S T A K E ■ ■
S O L E M N ■ C O H O ■ N A E
A W A R E ■ S O L I ■ E D A M
B I N G ■ A N T I C ■ C O L E
E N D S ■ R E A D ■ R O U T E
R G S ■ A T E N ■ C E N S O R
■ C A V E R ■ G A M ■ ■
G R A Z E S ■ C A V A L I E R
R A P T ■ I N C L I N A B L E
I S E E ■ A S C O T ■ R I E L
M A S C ■ N A P P Y ■ D D A Y
```

Answer 69

A	R	C	A		A	S	C	A	P		A	C	A	D
C	U	R	B		L	H	A	S	A		S	A	V	E
N	E	O	L	I	B	E	R	A	L		A	R	I	L
E	S	P	E	C	I	A	L		M	O	H	A	V	E
				I	N	F		C	L	A	I	M		
P	O	M	E	L	O		S	U	I	T		E	L	S
H	O	A	R	Y		G	E	E	K		P	L	A	N
A	Z	A	N		A	U	D	I	E		L	I	S	I
S	E	S	S		S	E	A	N		B	I	Z	E	T
E	S	T		A	S	S	N		F	L	E	E	R	S
		R	A	B	A	T		L	O	A				
A	M	I	D	E	S		M	I	S	S	I	L	E	S
N	A	C	L		S	H	O	E	S	T	R	I	N	G
A	G	H	A		I	M	A	G	E		E	M	I	T
S	E	T	I		N	O	N	E	S		D	A	D	S

Answer 70

T	A	B	S		K	N	O	C	K		A	B	I	E
A	I	R	Y		N	A	D	I	A		L	O	S	S
C	R	E	S	C	E	N	D	O	S		C	O	L	T
H	E	A	T	H	E	N	S		H	O	O	K	E	D
			E	L	Y		S	M	E	A	R			
A	B	B	E	S	S		R	E	I	D		E	S	P
R	E	E	L	S		G	E	A	R		O	V	A	L
A	R	E	O		C	A	C	T	I		H	I	L	O
B	E	R	N		A	M	A	S		K	N	E	A	D
S	A	G		S	N	A	P		C	R	O	W	D	S
		A	C	I	D	Y		D	O	O				
B	A	R	L	E	Y		C	I	N	N	A	B	A	R
L	I	D	O		A	C	R	O	M	E	G	A	L	Y
E	D	E	N		S	A	U	N	A		A	D	E	E
B	A	N	E		S	T	E	E	N		L	E	S	S

Answer 71

B	E	A	M		L	A	S	S	O		A	A	R	P
A	P	I	A		O	B	O	E	S		C	R	E	E
R	E	D	I	S	C	O	U	N	T		O	R	N	E
K	E	E	L	H	A	U	L		E	S	C	H	E	R
		A	L	T		R	I	S	K	Y				
F	A	C	A	D	E		L	I	T	E		T	A	B
O	V	A	T	E		S	I	S	I		G	H	E	E
N	E	M	O		H	I	C	K	S		A	M	O	R
D	R	O	P		A	S	I	S		F	E	I	N	T
A	S	U		M	C	A	T		C	A	L	A	S	H
		F	R	A	I	L		C	I	R				
P	A	L	A	C	E		D	U	N	G	A	R	E	E
A	C	A	D		N	E	E	R	D	O	W	E	L	L
A	L	G	A		D	E	L	V	E		E	N	O	L
R	U	E	R		A	L	T	E	R		E	O	N	S

Answer 72

O	A	F	S		P	R	I	G	S		S	D	A	K
A	G	R	O		R	E	V	U	E		P	A	G	O
R	E	A	F	F	O	R	E	S	T		A	R	O	N
S	E	N	T	A	W	A	Y		B	A	D	E	G	G
			D	A	N		F	A	C	E	D			
D	I	P	P	E	R		H	A	C	K		E	D	O
E	R	R	E	D		R	A	C	K		A	V	O	N
E	K	E	D		D	O	R	I	S		L	I	L	I
R	E	C	S		O	S	S	A		D	E	L	C	O
E	D	A		H	U	S	H		L	E	S	S	E	N
		R	A	B	B	I		C	E	P				
S	P	I	G	O	T		D	I	V	O	R	C	E	E
P	O	O	L		E	L	E	V	A	T	I	O	N	S
C	L	U	E		R	A	N	I	N		A	S	I	S
A	S	S	T		S	M	E	L	T		L	A	D	E

Answer 73

H	A	A	G	■	S	O	A	M	I	■	B	O	L	L
I	S	A	R	■	E	L	I	A	N	■	A	S	I	A
C	H	R	I	S	T	E	N	E	D	■	A	T	A	T
K	E	E	P	A	T	I	T	■	E	M	E	E	R	S
■	■	N	E	C	■	A	M	A	D	O	■	■	■	■
S	H	R	I	K	E	■	D	R	A	B	■	B	B	C
H	Y	E	N	A	■	R	A	I	N	■	S	L	O	E
I	P	S	A	■	S	I	R	E	D	■	C	A	R	A
N	O	E	S	■	A	C	I	S	■	B	A	S	E	S
S	S	A	■	M	P	A	A	■	C	E	N	T	R	E
■	■	R	E	S	I	N	■	A	R	E	■	■	■	■
E	N	C	A	G	E	■	B	R	A	C	K	I	S	H
R	A	H	S	■	N	O	T	A	C	H	A	N	C	E
I	L	E	T	■	C	H	U	C	K	■	N	C	A	R
C	A	D	S	■	E	S	S	E	S	■	S	A	D	A

Answer 74

L	E	A	D	■	J	A	D	E	S	■	A	C	H	E
E	S	T	O	■	A	G	A	M	A	■	G	O	A	L
A	S	T	I	G	M	A	T	I	C	■	A	U	R	A
H	E	A	T	H	E	N	S	■	R	H	I	N	A	L
■	■	■	■	A	S	A	■	S	E	A	N	S	■	■
A	R	M	A	N	I	■	M	A	D	D	■	E	S	A
K	O	A	L	A	■	C	A	R	L	■	E	L	H	I
I	T	S	O	■	C	O	C	K	Y	■	S	L	U	M
N	A	S	T	■	A	A	H	S	■	A	T	O	N	E
S	S	A	■	O	N	T	O	■	S	P	A	R	S	E
■	■	S	A	U	D	I	■	M	E	R	■	■	■	■
B	E	A	U	T	Y	■	F	A	C	E	L	E	S	S
A	M	U	R	■	A	L	O	H	A	S	T	A	T	E
R	I	G	A	■	S	I	R	E	N	■	D	R	A	W
B	L	A	S	■	S	M	A	R	T	■	S	S	T	S

Answer 75

L	I	M	B	■	R	O	P	E	D	■	S	H	A	D
A	D	U	E	■	A	G	I	L	E	■	P	A	T	E
B	O	T	T	O	M	L	E	S	S	■	E	R	I	E
S	L	E	E	P	I	E	R	■	C	R	A	M	P	S
■	■	R	F	D	■	S	E	I	K	O	■	■	■	■
M	I	D	D	A	Y	■	B	A	N	C	■	N	S	A
O	B	E	A	H	■	H	A	R	D	■	R	I	I	S
A	S	C	H	■	P	A	N	G	S	■	D	O	N	S
N	E	L	L	■	R	U	N	E	■	S	A	U	C	E
S	N	A	■	B	O	T	S	■	B	A	S	S	E	T
■	■	S	O	A	V	E	■	R	E	V	■	■	■	■
H	A	S	B	R	O	■	L	O	V	E	A	B	L	E
A	L	I	I	■	K	H	Y	B	E	R	P	A	S	S
L	I	F	E	■	E	A	S	E	L	■	A	B	A	T
S	A	Y	S	■	D	R	E	S	S	■	R	E	T	S

Imprint
Tim Rosenbladt
Carissa, Block 14, Flat 7A
Triq F. Vidal, Ibrag
SWQ 2471, Malta

Puzzles are created using Crossword Express